The Abracadabra Effect

Chick Moorman and Thomas Haller

Personal Power Press
Merrill, Michigan

The Abracadabra Effect

Library of Congress Catalogue Card Number: 2014947776

ISBN: 978-0-9821568-5-8

Printed in the United States of America

Personal Power Press
P.O. Box 547
Merrill, MI 48637

Cover Design
Parker Haller
www.parkerhaller.com

Table of Contents

Introduction

The Abracadabra Effect makes the case that the world is sick. It is suffering profusely and getting sicker. Most people sense something is wrong with their world, your world, and *the* world, but many of them remain unconscious about the nature of this sickness and what to do about it.

Maybe you don't believe this is a sick world. Perhaps you don't think we all could use some degree of healing. Look around you. Notice the people in your life where you live, work, play. Most of you will see marriages in shambles or people living with a partner they wish they weren't with. You may see a child out of control or a neighbor struggling with a career they don't want. You might notice people with a life in disarray, feeling stuck, frustrated, or unfulfilled.

It's time to learn about what we've identified as the "Abracadabra Effect": how it works and how to use it to benefit the general health of us all.

Listen to the people around you. You will hear evidence that we have become a world of complainers, blamers, and disowners. Many of us talk as if we have no control over our own thoughts, beliefs, or actions. We speak as if we are entitled to have what others have, regardless of our involvement in obtaining or maintaining it. We act and sound like victims.

It's beyond time to put the Abracadabra Effect to work to heal the planet and ourselves.

The 13 verbally transmitted diseases detailed in the pages that follow have worked their way into our occupations, our schools, our homes, and even our leisure-time activities. We have all seen the results. The dis-ease these diseases produce manifests in a partner who denies the effects of his or her infidelity on their primary relationship, a coworker who blames others for her mistakes, and a public official who promises one thing and does another. The results of this dis-ease show up in the teacher or administrator who shames and ridicules students, a parent who doesn't set healthy limits with his children, or a college student believing her professor is responsible for her low grade.

Look at the increasing number of people who are obese. Notice the number of men who hit their wives or girlfriends each year. Road rage, gossip, child abuse, and stress-related disorders abound. Countless numbers of people solve problems with power and force instead of negotiation and encouragement. Substance abuse and smoking cigarettes with warnings on the package are further indications that the lack of health is prevalent today and increasing. Examine your own medicine cabinet.

Perhaps you've heard children make excuses instead of making amends. Probably you have seen them or their parents cut corners, ignore rules, judge others, and stay unconscious of how their choices affect others. Many young people sit on a couch, drink soda, eat chips, and play video games for a good portion of the day. It is no accident that it often takes thirty years to create a twenty-year-old.

Guess what? It's time to use the Abracadabra Effect for the benefit of all.

This book will make the case that we are indeed living in a world of dis-ease. That world is one in which we continuously use the Abracadabra Effect to infect each other, our children, and ourselves without even knowing it. Current infections are being passed from person to person and back again. Our personal dis-ease reinforces the dis-ease of others and cycles back to us. This lack of wellness is being handed down through the generations. Sadly, in our opinion, the disorders are growing stronger, continually affecting our physical, emotional, and mental health, both as individuals and as a society.

In *The Abracadabra Effect* we describe the infectious nature of 13 invisible maladies and detail ways to prevent and/or cure them. This book will describe ways we inflict sickness on ourselves by robbing ourselves of joy, harmony, peace, well-being, self-esteem, love, and an active sense of personal power.

In the Preamble, the Abracadabra Effect will be defined and explained. Here we show how this powerful effect has helped us create the dis-ease that permeates our culture and how that same effect can be used to eliminate it. Are you tempted to read ahead to find out what the Abracadabra Effect is? If you're waiting for our permission, you are already creating dis-ease for yourself. Seriously.

Chapter 1 describes how our language patterns—how we speak—spread dis-ease through our culture in unsuspecting ways. In this chapter we demonstrate the importance of the everyday words and phrases we use as well as the necessity for vigilance in our choice of language. We explain why our style of language is the perfect carrier for dis-ease and make the case that it is difficult to detect. Because dis-ease is embedded deeply in our familiar language patterns, most of us remain unconscious about the role we play as carriers and spreaders of sickness in our world.

Chapter 2 shows how the seemingly innocent phrases "makes me" and "made me" rob us of our understanding of how the world really works. It reveals how this language affects our thinking and ultimately influences our behavior, creating a major disconnect between our view of the world and a sane path to emotionally healthy living. The major disease, which we describe as the "Makes Me" Psychosis, invades our thought process, worms its way into our belief system, and shows up later in our lives as a lack of responsible behavior.

Chapter 3 reveals a wide range of alternative delivery systems for the "Makes Me" Psychosis that has reached epidemic proportions in the world today. Common language patterns carry and promote this dis-ease and many of them are exposed here. Strategies for preventing and curing this sickness are also presented.

Chapter 4 takes you on a trip into the future to look and listen to what it would be like to live in a world free of the "Makes Me" Psychosis. It compares and contrasts the dis-ease we are currently creating using the Abracadabra Effect with what optimum health would look like and sound like if we used that same effect to provide a cure.

Chapter 5 offers a clear description of how we limit ourselves and give our power away by using self-limiting language patterns. This serious infection, which we call "Unableism," invades the subconscious mind, is reinforced through repetition, and affects our beliefs about ourselves. Later, it manifests in ways that evade our conscious recognition.

A plethora of "I can't" variations is examined in Chapter 6. Here you will learn whether you put yourself at dis-ease by creating imaginary and often unrecognized limits that affect your behavioral choices. Do your language patterns choke off possibility in your life? Are you suffering from Unableism without even knowing it? You will find out here.

Chapter 7 details the self-limiting, rationalizing, preventing, defensive ways we use the word "too" to create the dis-ease of "Preventarrhea" in our lives and the lives of others. This section will explain how "too," if used regularly, structures our beliefs and alters our behavior in unhealthy, dysfunctional ways.

Preventarrhea continues in Chapter 8 and Chapter 9. Little-known strands of this disease will be exposed so they can be subjected to rigorous treatment. "Dead Enders" and the use of "but," both highly contagious forms of Preventarrhea, may be unknowingly binding you and preventing you from reaching your potential.

Chapter 10 shares the language forms and effects of "shoulding" on ourselves and others. "Have to," "got to," "should," "should have" and similar verbal expressions create the discomfort of time urgency and anxiety while reducing our effectiveness and sense of personal power. "Shoulditus" is the diagnosis. Choose here from several prescriptions designed to combat it.

Chapter 11 contains information on how we were taught to rate, rank, and evaluate and have become unsuspectingly ensnarled in the judgment trap. Without our conscious awareness or full consent, comparison and the rating game have become a way of life, and most of us aren't even aware of how debilitating its confining influence is. This dis-ease, "Judgmentalillness," limits our vision and narrows our perspective in ways that lead us into the unhealthy beliefs of superiority and inferiority.

"The Rightabolic Syndrome" is the focus of Chapter 12. Here we reveal a common dis-ease that helps us feel good about ourselves temporarily. Long term, however, needing to be right doesn't work. A preoccupation with being right distances us from others. This "better than" stance is one more way we get to feel superior at the expense of others and sabotage our own emotional, mental, and physical health.

Chapter 13 exposes the game of "Blameopoly" as one more way we use language to spread dis-ease by assigning responsibility to someone or something else for the present conditions in our lives. Blame is a common technique that keeps responsibility off our own backs, a strategy for which we pay a heavy price in terms of mental and emotional well-being. When we use it, we give up our power, render ourselves impotent, and leave others in control. In short, we diminish our ability to be response-able people.

Chapter 14 describes a condition called "Needatonin" that pushes our heart's desires further from our own grasp. Needing, longing, and hoping are symptoms of this dis-ease which functions to keep us stuck in a place of perceived need while keeping attainment securely at arm's length. This silent consciousness invader often does its infectious work without our permission or awareness.

"Fungatious Feedback," described in Chapter 15, shows how indiscriminate praise can be unhealthy, harmful, and even destructive to us, our relationships, and our world. You might be surprised to learn that the most commonly used style of praise often works like a drug, producing praise junkies. In this chapter you will be exposed to a style of praise that leaves the recipient in control of the evaluation and the conclusion.

"Corrective Fungatious Feedback" is the main theme of Chapter 16. You will learn that criticism is fungatious. It creates disabling distance between people. It does not work to move an employee, friend, or family member forward. Instead of feeding forward, it feeds stuck. This chapter presents a style for giving corrective feedback that is free of dis-ease-spreading agents and is likely to be heard and acted upon.

Chapter 17 concentrates on "Personal Fungatious Feedback." Here you will be able to determine the health of your self-feedback. Do you provide feedback to yourself in a dis-eased way, making it less likely that you will choose positive action steps? Or do you send healthful messages to yourself that eliminate dis-ease progression and move you toward self-responsibility, confidence, and personal power? Find out here.

A condition that leads to regular impairment of present-moment living, "Presentphobia," is covered in Chapter 18. Two related symptoms of this illness are the "Someday Soon Syndrome" and "Pasting." Victims of the Someday Soon Syndrome sabotage their present moments by delaying action until later. Procrastination or postponing produces endless suffering and misery. Lethargy and inaction are often the debilitating results of this dreaded condition.

Pasting, the other side of the Someday Soon Syndrome, keeps us attached to the past and ineffective in the present. The language of regret keeps us focused on opportunities lost and blinds us to those that exist now. Our eyesight suffers because of the blinders we create with both forms of avoidance of present-moment living.

Chapter 19, "Degenerative Confidence," helps you determine your level of confidence. Is it robust and healthy, ready to serve you in energized ways, or is it weak and diminished through neglect and dis-ease? Take the eighteen-question confidence quiz to find out. Make the necessary corrections and you are on your way to a healthy, maximized belief in yourself.

You may have noticed that we have used the word dis-ease in many instances in this introduction. We will continue to do that throughout the pages that follow. Disease, a condition that impairs normal functioning, often invites us to be at dis-ease; that is, uncomfortable, stressed, anxious, irritated, or violent. Likewise, stress, anxiety, irritation, and the like invite our bodies to be more receptive to disease. We believe there is a strong correlation between dis-ease and disease, so strong that we often use the words interchangeably.

The material for this book is drawn from our own experience, Thomas as a twenty-five-year psychotherapist and Chick as a fifty-year professional educator. We have been husbands, fathers, friends, and more. We coauthor and copresent. All of our life experiences have led us to this time and place. Our intention is not to create just another gentle self-help book that you can read and implement sporadically. Our goal is to invite you to shake yourself to your core, to bring you face-to-face with the notion that we are living in a dis-eased world that requires healing, to challenge you to leap out of your comfort zone and begin to do something about it immediately. If you change yourself, you change the world

You are the one. Today is the day. Now is the time. No more excuses. Read on.

The Abracadabra Effect Preamble

When Thomas was a youngster, he watched a woman on stage placed in a box. Only her head and legs were showing. She and the box were sawed in half by her partner, the lead performer. The two parts of the box were then separated so one contained her head and upper body and the other box, now five feet away, held her legs and lower body. Next, the box parts were placed behind a curtain. After uttering the word "Abracadabra," the performer pulled back the curtain and there stood the woman, quite intact. The audience responded with applause.

Chick recalls a similar incident in his early life. As a first grader, he attended a school magic show. The magician took off his silk hat, tapped it repeatedly with a baton, and held it out for the children to examine. Chick verifies that the hat was empty. The performer then tapped the empty hat three more times and said . . . Can you feel it coming? All together now . . . ,

"Abracadabra." He then reached into the hat and pulled out a big rabbit. Chick's jaw dropped open.

Situations like these are common when it comes to experiences involving the word "abracadabra." Most of you, as we once did, probably associate the word with the performance of some magic act. To this day, in our minds the word still has a magical flavor to it.

In this moment you might be thinking, "This is a book about magic." Maybe. Maybe not. Neither of us believes in magic—except we do. There is nothing magical about this book at all—except there is. It all depends on how you define magic.

Consider abracadabra's roots. Were you aware that "abracadabra" is actually a Hebrew phrase meaning, "I create what I speak"?

"I'm going to place this broken woman behind this curtain and when I open it she will come out whole." *Abracadabra.* (I create what I speak.)

"I am going to pull a rabbit from this hat." *Abracadabra.* (I create what I speak.)

What if the concept of abracadabra is accurate? What if we *do* create what we speak? What if our words *are* magic? What if we are all magicians and don't know it?

The magicians in our childhood used illusions to create what they spoke. Our belief, described in detail in *The Abracadabra Effect*, makes the case that our language patterns, our repetitious thought, and the resulting beliefs we come to hold create the reality we produce in our lives. Only in this case, it is not only our audience that is fooled by the illusions. We the performer, the perpetrator of the illusions, do not even know why or how we produce the results we generate. We don't even understand the magic we are doing or not doing to ourselves. We are still trapped in our own illusions that we ourselves have created.

Are you ready to be free of illusions? Are you ready to create magical results in your life? Your magic wands await you. They are described on the pages that follow. When you learn to use them regularly, you will put the Abracadabra Effect to work on your behalf, producing more personal power, responsibility, creativity, health, energy, persistence, or any other positive attribute you desire.

One more thing: your magic wands aren't really magic—except they are.

Abracadabra.

Chapter 1
The Delivery System

"Hello, newborn. Welcome to the English language, separating you from self-responsible living, beginning the day you were born."

Mary Ann waited until she was forty-one years old to have her first child. Her labor was long and hard, fourteen hours in all. One nurse, who began working with Mary Ann as soon as she was admitted, went off duty before the child was born. When the nurse returned to duty the following day, she entered the hospital room, went straight to the baby, picked him up and announced, "So there you are, Mr. Stubborn. You gave everybody a lot of trouble last night. Just a stubborn little cuss, aren't you?"

And so it began for this baby, held in loving arms, wrapped with loving intentions, while being quickly infected with a dis-ease that could go undetected his entire life.

This child is not alone. Most of us were born into a culture that thrives on labeling, blaming, shaming., making others wrong, judging, disowning and taking the victim stance. In short, at birth we enter a dis-eased society. Being a newborn, we are not conscious of the fact that many of the adults we will encounter share an important characteristic with us. They too are unconscious and unaware. They don't realize they are spreading an infection that could severely limit our sense of personal power and the degree of personal responsibility we will later display in our lives.

Somewhere between birth and this present moment you figured out that language was a medium of communication. You learned to say "no," "mine," "eat," "Mommy," "up" and other words that helped you obtain what you wanted. You learned that the use of language could change your life for the better. So you kept learning words to continually improve the quality of your life. Little did you realize, at that early stage of your life, that many of those same words would soon be doing considerable damage to the quality of your time on earth.

You probably didn't realize that some of the words you mastered were infected. Some of the primary language patterns you heard and repeated were tainted with dis-ease in the form of guilt, worry, anxiety, fear, tension, shame, limitation, and dependence. Those unhealthy language patterns shaped your perception of the world, helped create your beliefs, and eventually influenced your actions. Some of the beliefs you hold today and the actions you take are a direct result of the words you learned to speak at an early age, before you knew better.

A major premise of this book is that language is more than a medium of communication. It is also a medium of perception. Our language patterns create mental constructs

through which we come to view the world. T
that limit our view of the world, walls that
through or climb over. They form, alter, and
perceive reality.

If your native language contains a hundred words for love, you will likely come to perceive and believe different things about love than will a person raised in a culture that has only three words to communicate the concept of love. You will think differently about love because you have more words to support your thoughts about it. You will develop different beliefs about love partly because you have developed a mental construct that can hold and support your belief system. Another factor is repetitious thought. The more you think a certain way about love or any other concept, the stronger your beliefs become. Eventually, your behaviors will flow out of your beliefs.

In short, if you speak one set of words, you see the world one way. If you speak a different set of words, you see the world a different way. Does that sound simplistic to you? Perhaps it is simplistic—so simple and so subtle, in fact, that many of us have trouble seeing the relationship between words and perception at all. We simply do not notice the connection between the words we use, the thoughts we think, the beliefs we develop, and the behaviors that flow from those beliefs. Because we don't perceive the relationship between our language patterns and our behaviors, we stay blinded to the harm they can bring to our lives and the lives of others.

Perhaps a schematic drawing would help to clear up the important connection between the words we use and the behaviors we exhibit.

Our words are the beginning of how we perceive reality and ultimately structure our lives. They are the inputs that program our minds and enable us to think certain thoughts and develop certain beliefs. Our words and language patterns are the main building blocks we use to manage our minds. *Abracadabra.*

Let's begin with words.

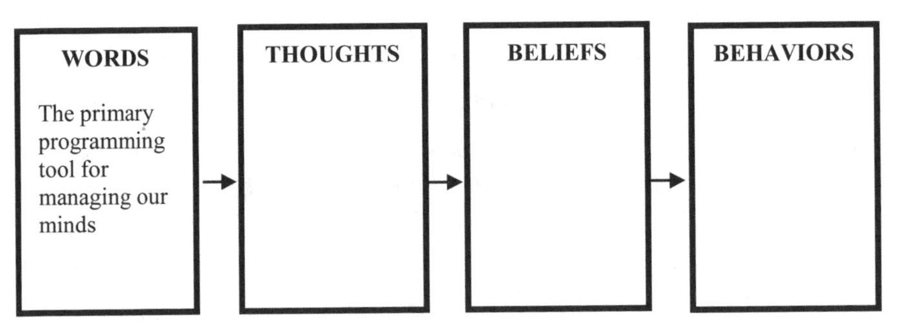

You are the writer, the director, and the computer programmer for your own mind, and words are your primary programming tool. Tools (words) can be used to create or destroy, to build or tear down, to uplift or push down, to create ease or dis-ease. If you use angry tools (words of rage and blame), you create an angry mind. If you use peaceful tools (words of gratitude and appreciation), you create a peaceful mind. Fill your mind with stressful tools (words of divisiveness and victimhood) and you produce a stressful mind. *Abracadabra.*

It takes words to think thoughts.

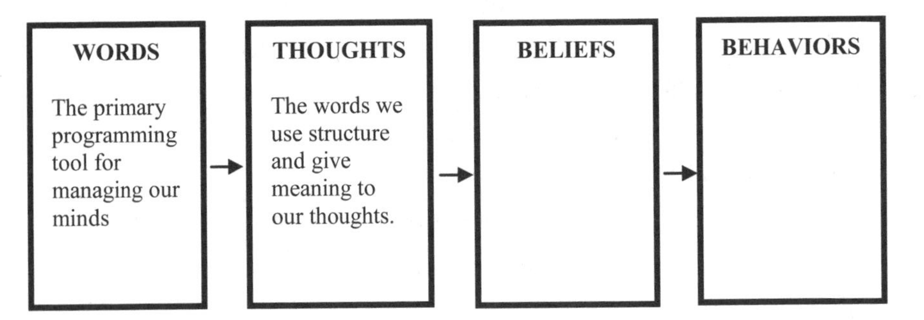

It takes self-responsible language to think self-responsible thoughts. Judgmental words form judgmental thoughts. Self-limiting words lead to self-limiting thoughts. It takes positive words to think positive thoughts. If this does not seem true for you, take a moment and attempt to think positive thoughts using only negative words. It doesn't work, does it? The words you use reflecting self-doubt, fear, excitement, faith, health, or sickness form the content and meaning of your thoughts.

Think the same thoughts often and you create a belief. *Abracadabra*.

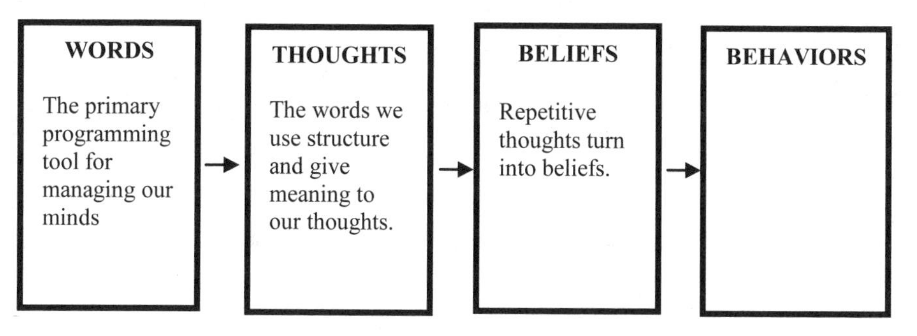

We know a young woman whose parents regularly teased her about their interpretation of her coordination. They called her "butter fingers" when she dropped a ball. Their favorite word for her was "klutz." They laughed when she tripped and often reminded (re-minded) her about her lack of coordination.

This young woman began thinking about herself as being uncoordinated. If she tripped on something, she would say silently to herself, "Oh, what a klutz." If she spilled a drink or food or dropped her phone, she might be heard saying, "Klutzy me." With enough repetition of klutz-related thoughts and language coming from both her parents and herself, she eventually came to believe she was uncoordinated.

Once she believed she was uncoordinated, she noticed more of her own behaviors that could be interpreted as uncoordinated. Unconsciously using this filtered selection process, in time she "proved" her belief to herself.

Her firmly held belief of herself as uncoordinated affected how she behaved. When we formed a coed softball team, we asked her to join. She declined, stating, "I'm not athletic." This woman was probably more athletic and coordinated than half the people participating in the program. Yet her belief about her own ability led to her action of choosing not to play. *Abracadabra.*

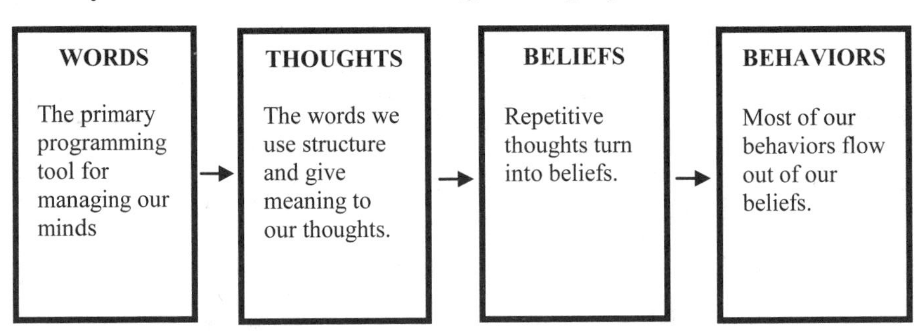

Simply stated, our words are used to create thoughts.

Thoughts, through repetition, turn into beliefs.

Beliefs influence our behaviors.

Almost like magic.

It all begins with words. Words, then, are the primary building blocks of our reality. If we want to unlock the secrets of our culture and cure the dis-ease that grips it, it's helpful to look closely at our language patterns—the words we use to communicate with one another and with ourselves. There we find the roots of the dis-ease that is continuing to infect the entire world population.

Words make minds. And it is the mind more than anything else that determines our mental and emotional health and the quality of our living. Your life is simply an extension of what you hold in your mind. Sooner or later, what you put in there—thoughts of sickness or health, lack or abundance, belief or doubt—will materialize.

Words are like seeds. You plant them in your mind and they take root and begin to grow. You nourish them with likeminded thoughts and allow them to strengthen and sink their roots deeper. Eventually, they sprout and turn into beliefs.

If you plant morning glory seeds, you grow morning glory plants. Planting watermelon seeds, no matter how often you weed, water, and fertilize them, will not result in morning glory plants. If you plant self-limiting seeds, you produce self-limiting beliefs. Sowing seeds that nourish self-acceptance results in self-enhancing beliefs. Unself-responsible seeds planted early and often by parents and caregivers end up producing adults who talk, think, believe, and act in unself-responsible ways. *Abracadabra.*

Your words and language patterns behave like hypnotic forces and make an impression on your subconscious mind. Your beliefs are continually being reinforced by the words you use when talking to yourself or to others. Plant enough impressions and you develop a belief.

You have seen this phenomenon in others. Have you ever noticed that teens who believe they are troublemakers make trouble, while teens who believe they are leaders act like leaders? Young children who believe they can read act like they can read. Children who believe they are slow learners behave like they are slow learners. Adults who believe they deserve to be treated respectfully act like they deserve to be treated respectfully. Adults who do not share that belief about themselves behave differently.

Once you develop a certain belief, you strengthen it by proving it to yourself through the process of filtered perception. Simply stated, we perceive what we have been programmed to see. What does not fit with our firmly held beliefs gets filtered out. We either don't notice it or we alter our interpretation of it so it is consistent with our current belief.

Talk is not cheap. As we will point out in the chapters that follow, talk is costly. The language of our culture, the language we were brought up with, the language we use without consciously choosing it, the language we hear on the radio and TV and view in magazines and on the internet, the language used in commercials and song lyrics, the language spoken by parents, teachers, coworkers, friends, relatives, and by ourselves is ripe with infection. Language is the primary spreading agent for dis-ease that manifests as stress, anxiety, doubt, judgment, criticism, gossip, insufficiency, limitation, depression, disowning, blaming, procrastination, regretting, shame, guilt, fear, self-rejection, ridicule, tension, unhappiness, nervousness, worry, compulsion, hurt feelings, anger, dependency, envy, jealousy, complaining, and more. It costs us immensely in terms of our emotional and mental health. In addition to the cost of pills, doctor visits, and hospital admissions, it costs us lost opportunities, leaves us with problems unsolved, unfulfilling relationships, and work that is void of mission or purpose. *Abracadabra.*

The most costly of all the sicknesses spread by the major dis-ease carrier (language) is the overriding lack of responsibility inherent in our culture. The vast majority of us do not speak, think, believe, or act self-responsibly. And until now that undetected sickness was being passed on quietly and secretly by 13 verbally transmitted dis-ease strains.

But no more. The 13 verbally transmitted dis-ease strains are hereby exposed. Read on.

Chapter 2
The "Makes Me" Psychosis

Call it Makesmeitus, the "Makes Me" Psychosis, Makesmeiteria or any other clever disease-sounding name you can think of. The specific name doesn't matter. What does matter is that most of us have unknowingly allowed "makes me" and "made me" to invade our language patterns and quietly spread dysfunction throughout our lives and the lives of other people we touch. Until now, their invasion and resulting damage have gone undetected. No more.

The "Makes Me" Psychosis defined: The repetitious use of "makes me" and "made me" that leaves you out of control and believing others are responsible for your attitudes and actions. A disowning of responsibility. A method for going unconscious and blaming others for your personal reactions to events and circumstances.

You hear the symptoms of this dis-ease often enough.

"Carlos *makes me* happy."

"Children *make me* anxious."

"That *makes me* proud."

"Don't you *make her* jealous."

"My boss *makes me* nervous."

"That *makes me* embarrassed."

"It *made me* extremely happy."

"You're gonna *make her* cry if you keep that up."

Every time we use a "makes me" phrase, we add to our disabling belief that someone or something else is responsible for our reactions to the people or events in our lives. This leads us to believe that someone or something else is in control of our responses to life. We disown our own personal reactions and assign cause to some other thing. Certainly not to ourselves.

One of the debilitating effects of this dis-ease is developing a diminished sense of personal power—so diminished that we don't even realize we are doing it to ourselves. Suppose you tell yourself that your wife or girlfriend can "make you" happy and she can "make you" sad. If she is in charge of your happiness and in charge of your sadness, what do you get to be in charge of? If she "makes you" sad and you want to be happy, you have to wait for her to change. There is not much personal power in waiting for her to alter her behavior before you can be happy.

"'Makes me' is just an innocent phrase," a workshop participant told us once. "We don't really mean that. It's just something we say."

Really? Tell that to the enraged man who is standing in front of his spouse yelling, "Don't you *make me* hit you!" That man believes in every cell of his body that his wife is making him hit her. The person who manifests road rage, the one who slaps her child, the one who shouts an obscenity, all believe *they* made them do it. Yes, they do.

This is pure sickness, and it permeates our culture. You can hear the symptoms in the lyrics of songs.

- "You *make me* feel like a natural woman."
- "Sunshine on my shoulders *makes me* happy."
- "You *make me* want to commit suicide, girl."
- "You *make me* want to *make you* mine."

Listen to the commercials that fill the air waves. They contain more evidence of the symptoms of this harmful dis-ease.

- "Our airline will *make you* feel like flying."
- "Chevy Chevette, it will *make you* happy."
- "You and Better Crocker can *bake someone* happy."
- "This movie will *make you* laugh."
- "This video game will *make* learning fun."

This dis-ease, the "Makes Me" Psychosis, travels a vicious path. It begins with the words "makes me" and "made me" and follows a route that leads steadily toward our behaviors, which eventually reveal more evidence of the damage of the dis-ease. Remember the schematic drawing in the previous chapter? When we choose to speak using the words "makes me" and "made me," those words structure our thoughts.

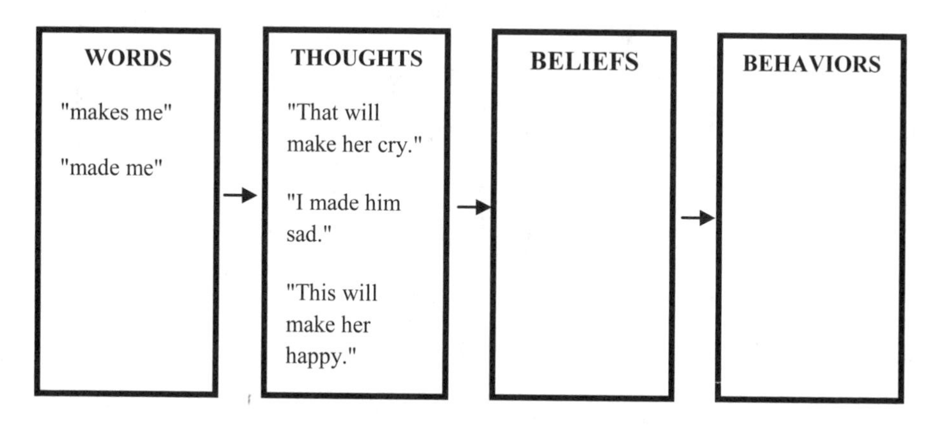

Repetitious thoughts turn into beliefs. After hearing and saying, "She made me mad," and other variations of this dis-ease often enough, we begin to believe she is responsible for making me mad. And why wouldn't we? Most people talk that way and sincerely believe others can make them feel or do something.

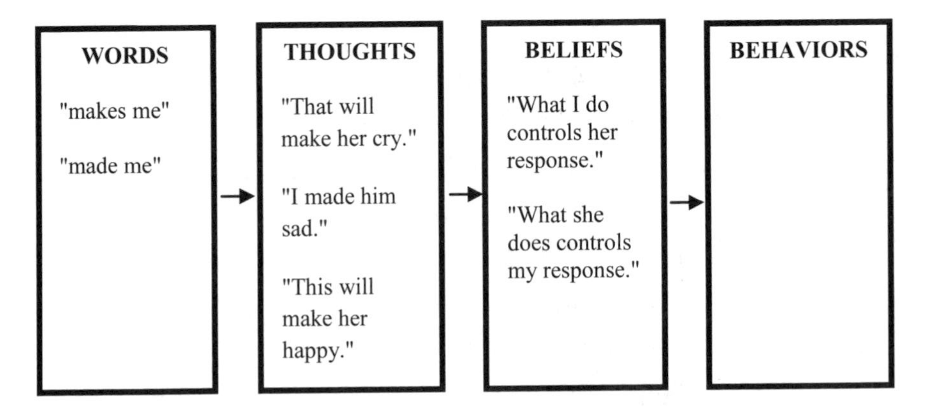

Once we internalize a belief that she *makes me* mad, many of our behaviors flow out of that belief. In other words, if I believe *she* makes me mad, I engage one set of behaviors. If I believe *I* make me mad, I'm likely to choose a different set of behaviors.

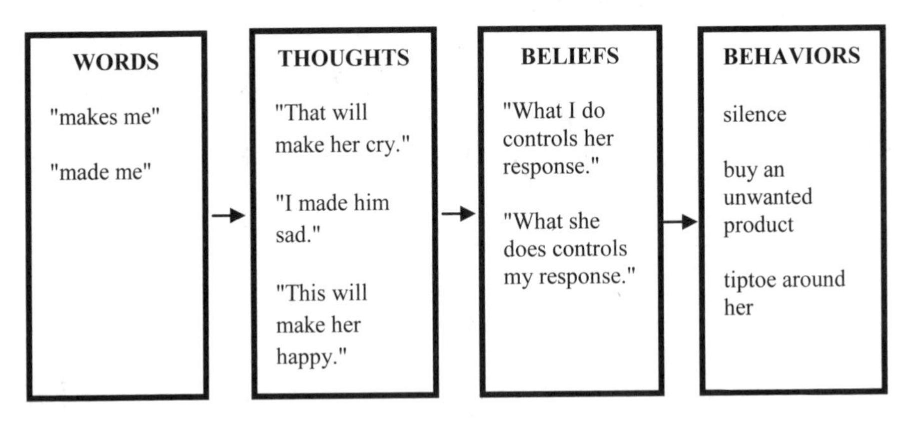

If I believe what you do influences my response, then I am more focused on your behavior than on my own. I look outward, at you, for relief, wishing you would change so I can stop being nervous. If I believe *I* control my response, then I am more likely to look inward for relief. I look to changing my thoughts and beliefs rather than focusing primarily on your behavior.

If I believe what I do controls your response, I am likely to choose behaviors designed to control your anger. (This would be a good time for us to wave a red flag and shout, **"Have you noticed how choosing behaviors to control others' anger doesn't seem to work very effectively?"**) This belief positions me as being responsible for your anger or happiness. On the other hand, if I believe it is your thoughts and beliefs that create your emotional state, then I see you as being responsible for your anger or happiness.

"You couldn't be more wrong about this" a workshop participant informed us early in a two-day seminar. "Traffic jams make me annoyed. If there is no traffic jam, I'm relaxed and peaceful. When there is a traffic jam, I get annoyed. No traffic equals calm. Lots of traffic equals annoyed. It's traffic jams that make me annoyed. I know that for a fact."

Not exactly. This thoughtful participant was missing one major component in his picture of what we call the "event/response model." Many people believe the event/response model works like this. An event happens and it leads to (creates) our response.

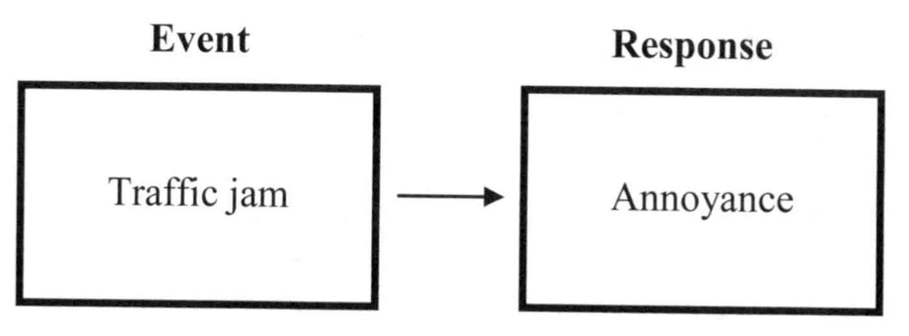

A morning traffic jam occurs, and I suspect I'm going to be late for a sales meeting. My response is annoyance. It sure appears as if the traffic jam "makes" me annoyed.

The same chart can be used to explain the following scenarios.

My boss gives me a tight deadline and it creates anxiety. (He makes me anxious.)

My child whines and that produces my irritation. (She makes me irritated.)

My girlfriend talks to another man at the party and that causes my jealousy. (She makes me jealous.)

These examples sound accurate enough and can be placed very neatly in the event/response boxes. They sure look like cause and effect in action. And, indeed, this is how "makes me" language comes into play. It's part of the illusion many of us live with.

But hold on! Something is missing here. Not all people react the same way when a traffic jam slows their drive to work. Not all employees get anxious in the presence of a tight deadline. Not all parents get irritated when a child whines. Not all men get jealous when their girlfriend talks to another man.

Let's take a closer look.

When an event occurs, there is a part of every human that gets triggered, gets put to work, becomes engaged. That is the part that gives meaning to the event. Although twenty people all see or experience the same event, they may derive vastly different meanings from it.

The part of us that becomes engaged is the missing link in the primitive event/response model on the previous page. It is the silent and real causative agent. It is the part that gives the event meaning. We call it "the interpretive mind."

What actually takes place when an event happens is a three-step process.

1. The person experiences an event.
2. His/her mind interprets that event.
3. He/she makes a response.

An accurate event/response model actually looks like this.

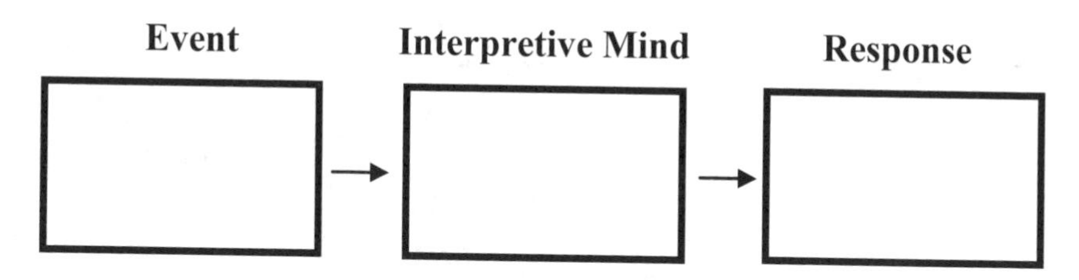

The interpretive mind functions in three ways to create a response to the events of a person's life. Responses to events are results of the interpretive mind ***thinking a thought***, ***creating an image,*** or ***engaging a belief.***

Let's go back to the traffic jam as an event and plug it into the now accurately revised event/response model.

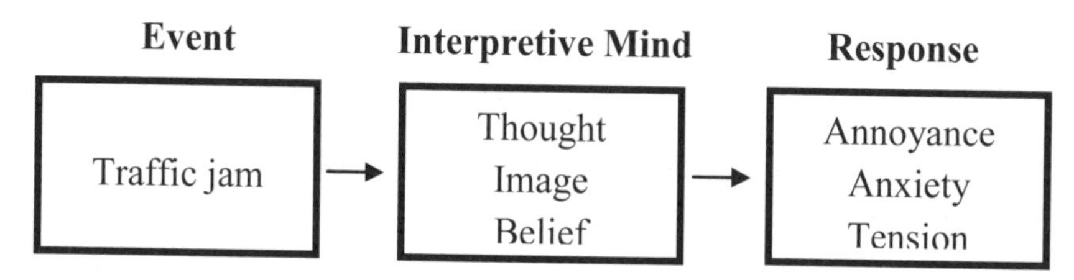

The traffic jam slowing my ride to work, ensuring I will be late for the morning sales meeting, is the event. Next, my mind interprets that event with a thought, image, or belief. If my thought is, "My boss isn't going to like this," my response could be annoyance. If I hold an image in my mind of the empty chair at the sales meeting and my boss looking at his watch several times, my response might be anxiety. If I have a belief that people should always be on time and that belief gets engaged, my response is likely to be tension and shallow breathing.

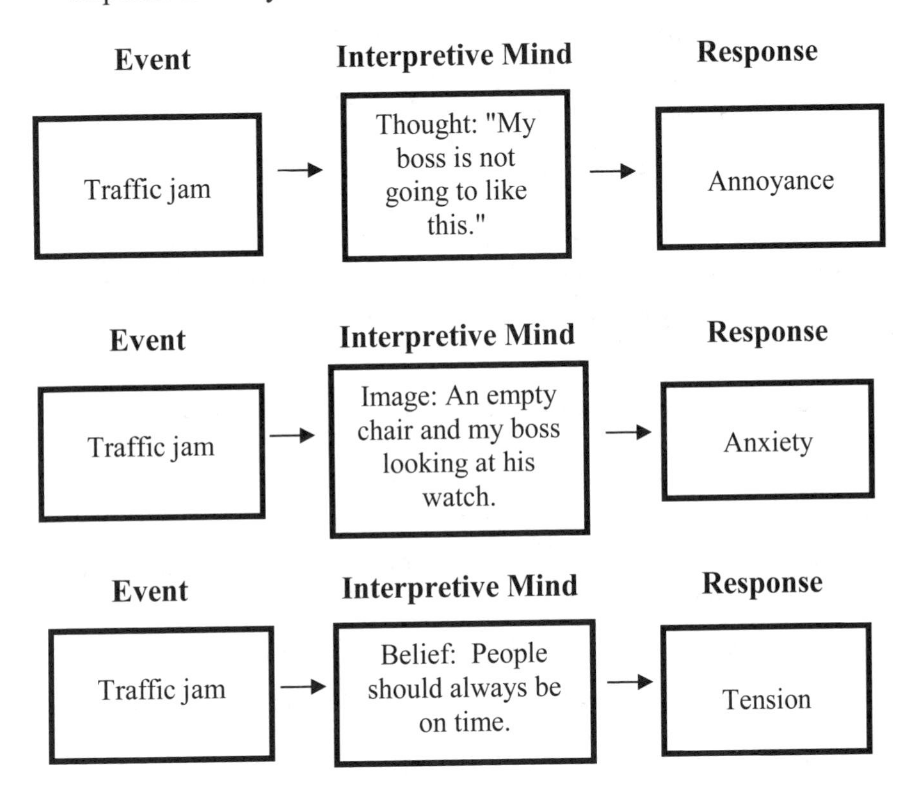

On the other hand, my mind can make a variety of other more helpful interpretations. I can elect to engage more useful thoughts, images, and/or beliefs.

My thought could be, "This traffic jam is a signal to me to slow down. I've been running a bit fast lately." If that's my thought, then my response could be to relax by doing some deep breathing or to feel appreciation that the universe reminded me to slow down for safety.

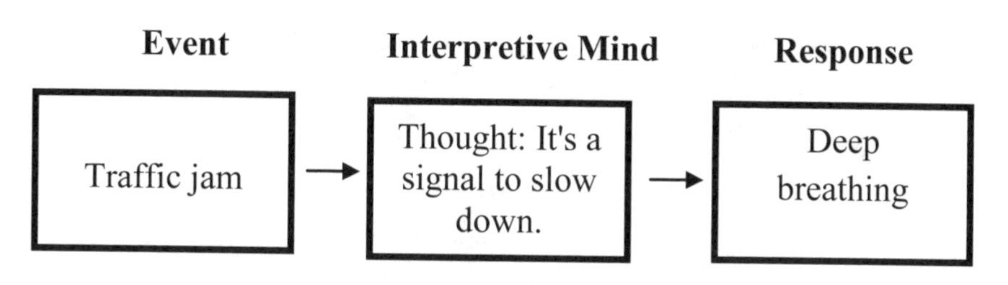

If my interpretive mind activates an image of others happily welcoming me when I do arrive, it could lead to a response of tuning into some soothing and relaxing music on the radio.

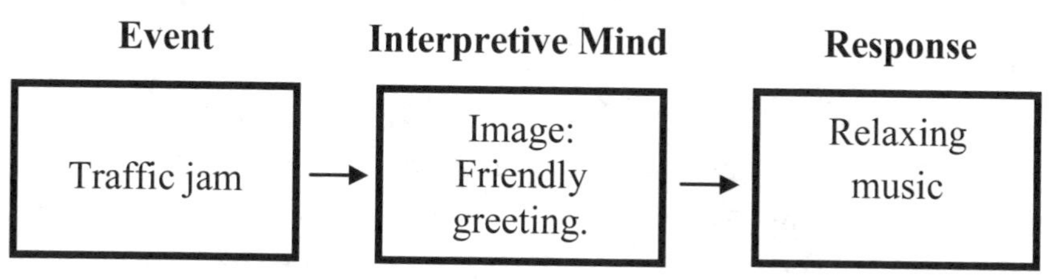

Perhaps one of my beliefs is, "What is, is and there is no sense in emotionally resisting what is." If that belief becomes engaged, then I choose a response like doing some isometric exercises or listing in my mind five things I intend to accomplish this day.

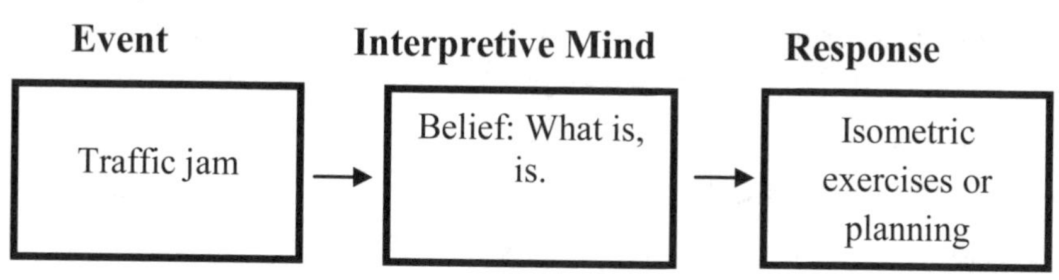

The point we want to emphasize here is that the event does not *cause* the response. *I* cause the response by a thought, image, and/or belief that *I* choose to hold onto in any given situation, and that is always *my* choice.

The traffic jam does not make me annoyed or elicit any other emotion. I make me annoyed by the thoughts I choose to think about the traffic. My boss giving me a tight deadline does not make me anxious. I make me anxious by the images I put in my mind or the thoughts I choose to think about the deadline. My child's whining does not make me irritated. I create irritation for myself because of how my mind interprets whining. My girlfriend talking to another man does not make me jealous. I create jealousness in myself because of how my mind interprets that incident. Each situation has no meaning until I give it one.

Because I am in control of the thoughts, images, and beliefs that are in my mind at any given time, I am in control of how I react to the events of my life. *It* doesn't make me. *I* make me.

This dis-ease, the "Makes Me" Psychosis, results in many people giving their power away. Mind you, their personal power is not taken away, nor ripped from their consciousness as they valiantly fight to hold onto it. No, they simply give it up voluntarily with no resistance or concern about it leaving. This invisible sickness is contracted unknowingly by people who were born into a culture whose language patterns support an English-speaking culture.

Now seems like a good time for us to communicate that we are not arguing against feeling angry, irritated, annoyed, happy, joyful, frustrated, or experiencing any other emotion. You get to be angry, annoyed, or have any feeling you think serves you in this moment. Just OWN it. Know that it is you, through your interpretive mind, that is creating the feeling in you, not some outside event, situation, or person. Know that it is your thoughts, images, and/or beliefs that are creating your interpretation, your present reality.

The Cure

The good news is, the "Makes Me" Psychosis can be controlled and even cured. And in that healing process, you can help keep the virus from being passed on and infecting others.

The bad news is you will need to pay for the cure. The prescription is free. The protocol for wellness, however, is expensive. The cure will cost you plenty.

Prescription 1

Here is the price you will have to pay. Attention. Yes, you will have to pay attention to your language patterns. And it is recommended that you pay often and pay regularly.

Awareness is the first step in moving toward a cure. Before you can move to something else, you have to be aware of what is now. To heighten your awareness, listen for "makes me" language this week. Keep a journal. Do the words come out of your mouth? Do you hear them in songs or commercials? Do you encounter them on the internet? Is there someone in your life who is using "makes me" language frequently? Pinpoint the primary places and people this sickness is coming from.

By paying attention, you may observe this verbally transmitted dis-ease coming from only a few people or situations or from many. If you become aware of situations or people that are likely to be infected, we recommend you decrease your exposure to this contagious malady by limiting your time in the vicinity of the likely spreaders. If you want to stay well, stay around people who use healthy language. Listen to music that promotes the language of wellness. Read healthy communications.

Prescription 2

Also, begin changing your own language. Use the pronoun "I" in front of "makes me." "*She* makes me jealous" then becomes "*I* make me jealous." "*Talking about sex* makes me feel embarrassed" is now "*I* make me feel embarrassed talking about sex."

Putting "I" in front of "makes me" puts you back in charge of your feelings and what you do with those feelings. "I make me" is an audible reminder of your personal power and the self-responsibility that actually exists in your life. You take ownership for your feelings and other responses to the events of your life.

Prescription 3

Another technique for reducing the power of the "Makes Me" Psychosis is to use the phrase, "I'm choosing."

"I'm choosing annoyance right now."

"I chose embarrassment when she brought that subject up."

"Right this moment, I am choosing to be angry."

Using the phrase "I'm choosing" is another way to remind yourself of the real role you play in activating your emotional responses. Speaking this way helps you stay conscious of your newly developing wellness. It helps you feel the full health effects of your increased options and sense of personal power. It keeps you from descending into a delusional spiral that convinces your unconscious self that you are not in charge.

Prescription 4

Another antidote to the "Makes Me" Psychosis is to simply report your feelings. Just state, "I feel angry," rather than, "You make me angry." Choose a language pattern that reminds you that you are in charge.

"I'm feeling sad."

"I'm excited."

"I feel irritated."

"I'm experiencing annoyance."

When you describe your feelings without the dis-eased "makes me" language, you are choosing healthy language that keeps you clear of this incapacitating illness. Your improving health benefits will include more personal power, more control, and more well-being for yourself and those around you.

Prescription 5

You will likely encounter others who are under the influence of the "Makes Me" Psychosis even if you work to limit your contact with them. In this case, we recommend you work on yourself rather than on them. While it is commendable to want to cure others of this dreaded dis-ease, this can be a formidable task and is best left in the hands of professional linguists. Chances are you are not a well-trained verbal health care provider. Remember, you are in an early process of recovery yourself, and that is enough responsibility for now. As much as you would like to, you cannot make other people better. The state of their health is a condition they will have to choose for themselves. The best way you can help others is to get well yourself and demonstrate the path to wellness in your words and actions.

When your partner, boss, neighbor, or acquaintance says, "You made me mad," refuse to hear that. Do not let it in. Instead, hear the speaker say, "I'm choosing to feel mad right now and I do not want to own it." Resist teaching a lesson. Resist arguing about who is really responsible for the feeling. Know that this person is in the midst of strong emotion. Simply congratulate yourself for noticing one of the symptoms of the "Makes Me" Psychosis and pat yourself on the back for the recognition.

"Why all the fuss over one phrase?" you might be wondering. "A little 'makes me' here and there doesn't really hurt anyone, does it?" Yes, it does.

Keep in mind, "makes me" is only one of 13 verbally transmitted diseases that are affecting the state of our health and well-being. In the following pages, we will describe many ways we unsuspectingly use language to rob ourselves of health, joy, self-esteem, harmony, accomplishment, love, and other positive health benefits.

However, we are not done with "makes me" yet! In the following chapter we will describe more negative outcomes of this style of language and the plethora of viral strands into which it has mutated. "She makes me" is only the beginning of identifying, isolating, and controlling this harmful dis-ease.

Chapter 3
"Makes Me" Variations

The way we talk about events, people, and situations needs to be overhauled to allow room for truth and the resulting wellness to surface.

"Makes me" language comes in a variety of shapes, forms, and intensities. The current deluge of unself-responsible language running rampant through our culture has greatly increased the size and strength of the "Makes Me" Psychosis, adding to the ever-growing illusion that other people and events control our responses. Many of the "makes me" mutations are subtle and difficult to detect. A sampling of some we have been able to isolate for examination and study are included here:

"It's frustrating me."

"You're embarrassing me."

"He changed my mind."

"Heights scare me."

"That offends me."

"This office staff is turning me into . . . "

"She ruined my life."

"She bothers me."

"He has my head spinning."

"He let me down."

"It just came over me."

"That pissed me off."

"He messed with my mind."

"My boss disappointed me."

"That is annoying."

"You turn me on."

"That's depressing."

"My manager stuck me with this report."

"You threw me with that one."

"Well, that ruins my mood."

"That's tying me up in knots."

"The customer put me on the spot."

"She turned my head."

"This job is driving me crazy."

"Young children wear me down."

"Don't get me started."

"He rubs me the wrong way."

"He broke my heart."

"She got me fired up."

"That is getting on my nerves."

"That gave me a complex."

"You lost me completely."

"She broke my trust."

"I had an anxiety attack."

"I lost my temper."

"He lights my fire."

"He swept me off my feet."

"He steered me wrong."

"You're killing me."

"She keeps stringing me along."

"My car just can't go by there without stopping."

"That irks me."

"He bores me."

"I'm OK. I know what to do when depression strikes."

"She got me going."

"It rubbed off on me."

"The mood overtook me."

"That brought me down in a hurry."

"She knows how to push my buttons."

"She brightened my day."

"My nerves are getting to me."

"He motivated me."

All of the preceding sentences are "makes me" in disguise. Each is an example of unhealthy language that diminishes your personal power and leaves someone or something else in control of your responses. Each requires you to look at what is happening around you rather than what is happening within you. Each effectively gives your power to outside forces over which you have little control. These verbal viruses travel rapidly through our language patterns, spread to our unconscious, invade our belief systems, and eventually limit our behavioral repertoire.

Some of us are sadly unaware of how sick we sound and how pronounced the "Makes Me" Psychosis really is in our lives. Take Marcy, for instance. She has three young children, all below the age of five. She firmly believes her two-and-a-half-year-old daughter often *ruins her day*. "It's her attitude," she explains. "She has to have everything she wants. If she doesn't get it, look out. It's whining and temper time. Fit city! If she wakes up in the morning in a bad mood, I know I'm going to have the worst day ever. *She just ruins* my whole day."

To our way of thinking, that's a lot of power to give to a young child. Why would anyone want to designate their preschool child as "person in charge" of an adult's attitude for an entire day? Why would anyone ever want to believe that a youngster can ruin even the beginning of the day, much less the whole day? "No one," is our quick response to those questions.

So if no one wants a young child to ruin their day, why would anyone allow it? The simple version of our answer is because they are sick, packed full of dis-eased thinking and beliefs. They are ill, bloated with infection, and suffering the real consequences of the "Makes Me" Psychosis. The bottom line is they lack awareness of their dis-ease so they know not what they do.

A more complicated answer is that most people in the culture where you were born speak unself-responsible language. Because that is the dominant style of speaking, people in your neighborhood (block, city, state, region, country) tend to think unself-responsibly as well. As we explained in chapter 2, words and thoughts are followed in lockstep by beliefs and behaviors. One big illusion many of us organize our lives around is that events and people can "make us" a whole bunch of things (sad, jealous, thrilled, depressed, and on ad infinitum). It's not true, of course. No one can "make us" anything. Still, many of us hang onto that illusion because it's more comfortable believing someone or something else is responsible for our feelings and actions than owning that responsibility ourselves. If *we* owned it, we might have to do something about it.

One indisputable fact that pertains to every strand of the "Makes Me" Psychosis is that the thoughts and beliefs that feed the dis-ease are simply not true. NOT ONE OF THEM. It's bad enough that this dis-ease encourages people to give up happiness, joy, responsibility, and emotional and mental health, as well as personal power. What is worse is that the dis-ease is all based on fiction. The language, thinking, and beliefs are simply incorrect.

Consider these statements:

"She ruins my day."

No, not correct. How Marcy in the previous situation thinks about her daughter's behavior, how she interprets that behavior, the meaning she assigns to it, and what she comes to believe about it is what ruins her day. She is, in effect, ruining her own day, all the while oblivious to the fact she is doing it to herself.

"It's frustrating me."

No, not correct either. *It* doesn't frustrate me. Whatever *it* is, it doesn't have the power to frustrate me. I can only do frustration to myself. I create my own frustration by the thoughts I choose to think and by how I choose to interpret *it*. So do you. The same goes for all of us.

"My manager offends me."

The truth is, people don't offend or annoy you. You can only do that to yourself. Being offended or being annoyed is your reaction and within your power to control. It is your unique personal response to another person, and you are in charge of that, not them.

Take manager M, for instance. Some people get scared around her. Some are happy. Others activate nervousness in her presence. Although it may be hard for you to believe, some people even get sexually aroused around manager M. Maybe not you, but others do. Some people get physically sick in her presence.

We all react differently to manager M. That being the case, is manager M responsible for all our diverse reactions? Is she really so powerful that she can make one person nervous, another excited, and still another frustrated, all in the same meeting? Nope. We all see her through different eyes, through different belief systems, through unique and individual life experiences. We each create our own perception of her, and our differing responses are a reflection of that. "My manager offends me" is simply incorrect.

"He pisses me off."

Take Hattie and Raul as an example. They've been married for twenty-five years. Notice we didn't say, "happily married." The marriage is unhealthy, to say the least. "Dysfunctional" might be a more accurate way to describe it. "Sick" would also suffice.

"He really pisses me off," Hattie confided to her counselor. "He drinks too much. He stays at the bar with his buddies rather than coming home. He pisses me off so much I can't stand being around him at night."

Raul counters, "She pisses me off so much I don't even want to be home. The minute I walk through the door she starts ragging on me and *making me* feel guilty. So I stay out longer and don't come home till late. She pisses me off big-time."

And the vicious cycle goes round and round.

At the risk of sounding redundant, no one can piss you off. You can only create pissed from the inside out. In this case, the incorrect language leads to blaming each other, with neither party looking seriously at how they contribute to the current situation. Both people are so engaged in defending themselves they do not hear what the other is unskillfully communicating: "I feel hurt and angry."

The infected language backed by contagious beliefs leads to unskilled expression of emotions and unhelpful behaviors. And the dis-ease perpetuates itself in the unsuspecting couple who still believe the other person is pissing them off.

You might be thinking, "Well, that's depressing." If so, hang on. Here comes your own personally designed, just for you, four-paragraph lecture burst.

"That's depressing."

Nothing is depressing unless you think it is depressing. There is no event, person, or situation that is depressing to everyone. There are only people and events that some of us interpret as depressing. Depression is not a thing. It is a process you engage in, something you do to yourself, internally.

We live in Michigan. It can get cold in the winter. A common refrain we hear in winter is, "This cold is so depressing. When is it going to warm up?"

No, cold is not depressing. It's just cold. "Well, it's twenty degrees Fahrenheit. That's depressing." Sorry. No sale. Twenty degrees is not depressing, either. It is just twenty degrees.

Chick's dad couldn't wait for the lakes to freeze over. He loved to ice fish. He didn't even use a shanty. He would bundle up in layers of clothes, drag his equipment box on a sled to a spot on the frozen lake that seemed right for him, spud a hole in the ice, and fish. He would sit on the wooden box, with his back to the wind, fishing for several hours. He was in fishermen's heaven. Cold was not depressing him. Hmm. Guess maybe it isn't cold that's depressing. Must once again be our own unique interpretations of cold.

"He trapped me in depression."

Bonita's husband attempted suicide. She found him at home unconscious but still breathing. She managed to get him to the hospital and stayed with him while the medical staff worked for hours to give him another opportunity to choose life.

Now, months later, with her husband doing well in recovery, Bonita is the one filled with anxiety. She worries a lot about finding him again, this time dead. She sleeps in, stays in bed as long as she can, afraid of what she will find when she gets up. Bonita lives a life of recurring depression. She is on medication to help her with her nerves. "*He stuck me* with this. *He trapped me* in depression," she often tells her friends.

Bonita recently began counseling to help her understand and cope with the situation. Our prediction is she will eventually be led to her own recovery through an understanding that her husband is not creating her depression. She will learn that her thoughts, images, and beliefs are the real cause of her depression. We suspect she will learn and use techniques for creating healthy language, thoughts, and beliefs that leave her in a place she likes, free of the "Makes Me" Psychosis.

"I'm OK. I know what to do when depression strikes."

We talk about depression as if it's on the other side of the hill, arming itself, getting ready to attack. We conceptualize it as something "out there," coming at us and harming us from the outside. Actually, most depression is an inside job caused by our thinking and beliefs. It's only the language we use that teaches us incorrectly that this is not so.

Depression Disclaimer: Please be advised that clinical depression—what is also called major depression—is a medical condition that affects millions of people every year. It is not our position that this type of depression is totally thought related. Major depression is treated effectively with medication. Antidepressants are a recommended treatment for major depression *along with* cognitive behavioral therapy (CBT).

An important aspect of CBT is the language a person uses, the thoughts they have, the beliefs under which they function, and the behaviors they demonstrate. Many doctors agree that psychotherapy or talk therapy that focuses on changing a person's thoughts, beliefs, and behaviors is a significant part of treating major depression.

The prescriptions we are suggesting here align with the treatment protocol recommended by many psychiatrists. We are encouraging psychotherapists and counselors who work regularly with individuals struggling with depression to focus on the specific words that are being spoken by their clients and to help them reframe and rephrase those words. You can also do much of this work on your own without a therapist. You can work on identifying and eliminating your unself-responsible, dis-ease-infected language.

"You're embarrassing me."

No one can embarrass you without your own consent. If you're embarrassed, it's because you bought into the idea. When you talk and think this way, you give your power to another person. They didn't take it from you. They didn't even need to ask for it. You just gave it to them.

"He let me down."

If he can let me down, then he must be in control of me. My choice of language here reflects a belief that he is in charge of my up/down buttons. When I believe he can let me down or lift me up, I have effectively given him the power to affect my up- or downness.

"He changed my mind."

No, he didn't. *You* changed your mind after listening to him speak for an hour. It's your mind. Why give him credit for changing something that belongs to you? There is much more personal power in "I chose to change my mind after listening to his ideas" than there is in "He changed my mind." Give yourself the credit and the power. After all, it is *your* mind.

"You lost me completely."

Really? You are the one who is lost, but someone else lost you? Own it. Use self-responsible language. "I'm lost. I don't understand. Will you explain that again?" Own that you didn't get it. Ask for help. Responsible behavior is more likely to follow when you choose self-responsible language.

"He bothers me."

Actually, you bother yourself by the interpretations you attach to what he does. If fact, he may be consciously attempting to bother you. If you don't bite the hook or are not preoccupied with thoughts about something else, you are not bothered.

Harmful Effects

The "Makes Me" Psychosis and its many mutations lead to a number of unhealthy effects. On a physical level, this disease manifests as anxiety, headaches, shallow breathing, high blood pressure, nervousness, and more. On an emotional level, anger, fear, sadness, boredom, depression, worry, unhappiness, dissatisfaction, and frustration can result. Behaviorally, spouse abuse, tantrums, name-calling, blaming, shaming, drug addiction, excuse-giving, overeating, smoking, and more can be attributed at least partially to the "Makes Me" Psychosis.

Not the least of the harmful effects of the "Makes Me" Psychosis is the loss of personal power and the decrease in choosing self-responsible behaviors.

The Remedies

Believing, thinking, and speaking in language such as "That annoys me" or "Salespeople offend me" is a waste of time and energy. It effectively prevents you from spending any effort examining what exists within you that reacts to the person or situation that way. It keeps you focused outward, away from yourself, away from where the sickness is festering. It points you instead toward someone or something you have little or no control over.

Prescription 1

When you notice a symptom (boredom, annoyance, anxiety, depression, joy, excitement, arousal, etc.), look inward for explanations and meaning. That is where health is created. That is where your power is. That is the key to your recovery and wellness.

When you hear yourself saying, “What a boring meeting,” it’s more helpful to ask, “Why am I choosing to bore myself?” than to continue to believe the meeting bores you. When you notice your self-talk is, “My wife’s eating those chips so loudly bothers me,” you will get more benefit from asking yourself, “What am I activating within me that won’t accept her not meeting my mental models of how a person eats appropriately?” rather than holding on to the illusion that she controls your reaction to chip munching.

Even if you don’t find answers to your questions, asking them will help you re-mind yourself that it is you who controls your reactions. You will then be more likely to choose a reaction (feeling or behavior) that fosters better health and leaves you feeling powerful and in control.

“Yeah, but she’s still smacking her lips while she eats those chips,” you might be thinking. “If she would just stop chewing that way, the problem would be solved.” Agreed. And your best hope of getting that to happen is to approach her knowing this is *your* problem, not *hers*. *She* is not bothered by the way she eats chips. *You* are. And since you now know you are bothering yourself with the chip eating and own that it is *you* who is bothering yourself, you have several options.

Let's return to the event/response model and check out the possible options that exist.

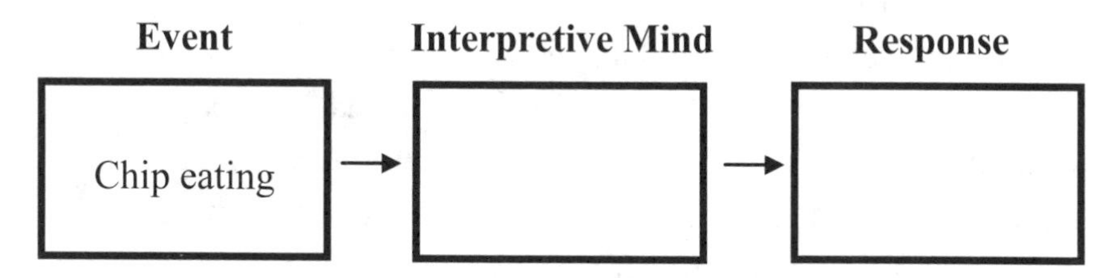

An event has shown up in your life. Your spouse is eating chips in a way that you are interpreting as annoying. You realize it is you who is creating the response through your interpretive mind. You are aware that your present inner response is annoyance.

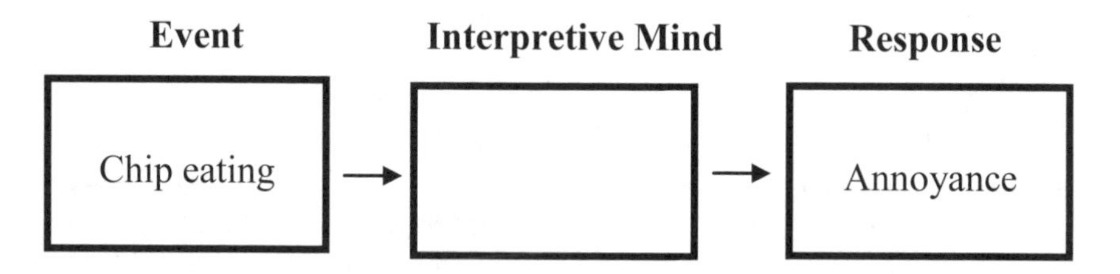

Working to change or eliminate the event is often appropriate and useful. One way you can choose to eliminate it from your consciousness is to physically remove yourself from where it's occurring. Go read your book in another room where chip eating is not occurring. That's one solution you can implement immediately to remove the problem you are creating for yourself with the chips. It requires no agreement or behavior change from your spouse. Now you have produced a new event, one that will probably not lead to annoyance. Not yours, anyway.

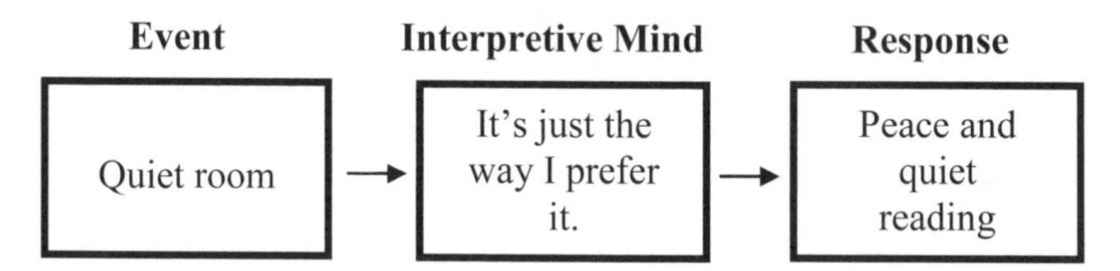

Or you can attempt to change the event by communicating with your wife. We are not against putting out to the universe the way you would like your world to be. Yes, go to her and explain *your* problem. Say, "Carmella, *I am creating annoyance for myself* listening to you chew. There is something in me that is preventing me from emotionally accepting chewing noise in this moment. How can we find a way to both get what we want?" When you speak that way, owning the problem, you stand a better chance of finding a healthy, mutually agreed upon solution than if you said, "That chewing is really annoying me. Knock it off!" or "Why can't you chew with your mouth closed?" Approached in a nonattacking manner, your spouse may be willing to alter her behavior, which also negates the necessity to move on to the interpretive mind phase of the event/response model.

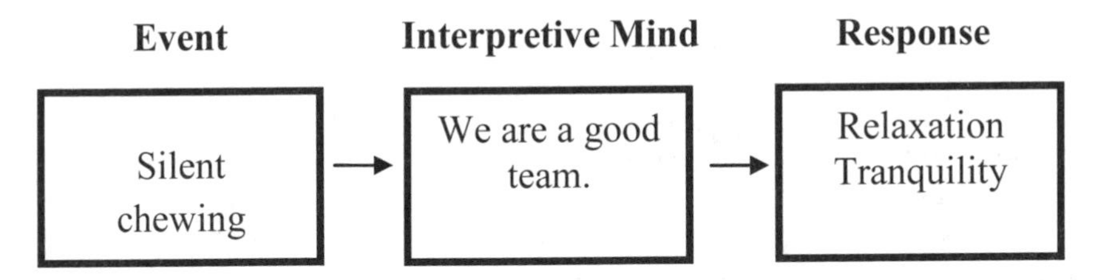

You won't always get what you want when you ask the universe to be exactly the way you want it to be. Both of us like to be talked to with self-responsible language. So we ask for that. Some of our close friends and relatives respect that desire and work hard to speak that way. Others do not. We cannot always control how someone talks to us even though we ask clearly and respectfully for it to be a certain way. How others talk to us is *their* choice, not *ours*. But one thing that is always in our power to control is what we say to ourselves about what they say to us. That is where the interpretive mind comes in.

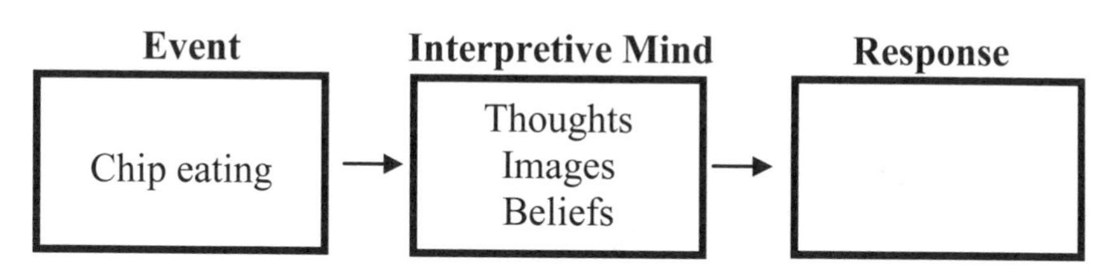

If you don't want to be annoyed and the chip chewing continues, you can change your thoughts, images, or beliefs about the situation. The thought, "She should be more careful about how she eats," can be replaced by, "I wonder why loudness increases eating enjoyment for her?" You might tell yourself, "She sure is having fun with those chips," or "The bag will be empty soon."

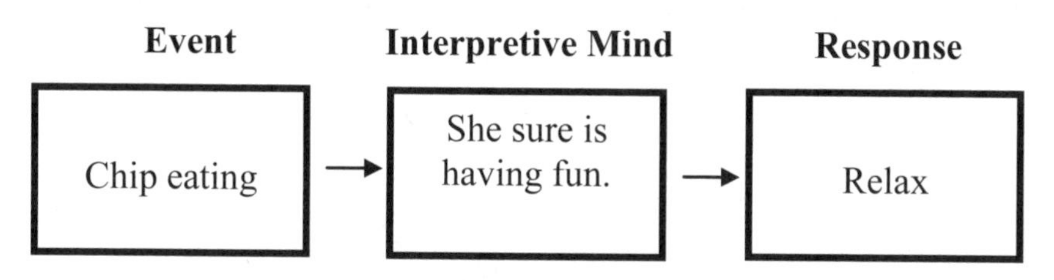

Change your image of a pig stuffing its face with slop to that of a loved one filling her body with peaceful contentment.

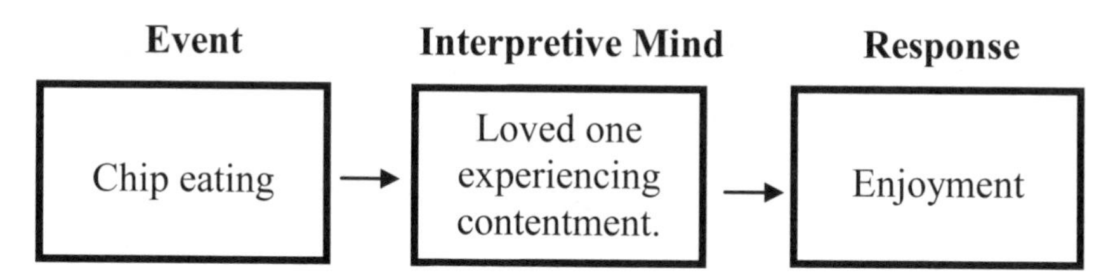

If your belief "People should always be aware of how they eat in front of others" becomes engaged, re-mind yourself, "People sometimes get so engrossed they don't realize how others are reacting."

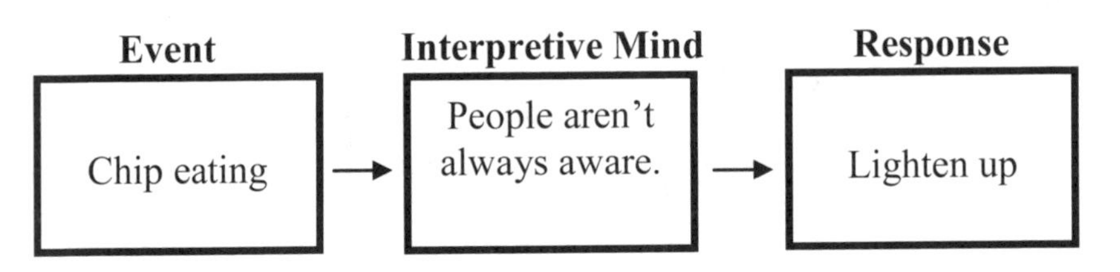

The options above are available to each of us in any situation. If you get stuck in a traffic jam, you can work diligently to change the event. Work to get in an exit lane. Exit as soon as you are able. Create another route to your destination. If changing the event is not possible, work to change your mind with calming thoughts, images, and beliefs. Each of these options is best implemented within the framework of knowing you are responsible for both your internal and external responses to the outside event.

There are times when working on changing the event is more important than modifying the thoughts of your interpretive mind. If your carpool partner is driving and exceeding the speed limit by twenty miles per hour, working on altering that event might be healthier than focusing on how your interpretive mind is processing it. If teenagers bring alcohol to your daughter's high school graduation party, understand that the situation is not making you mad. *And* work diligently and quickly to bring an end to that event.

Prescription 2

Repeat the following three prescriptions you used with "makes me" in chapter 2.

A. Pay attention to your language.
B. Use the pronoun "I".
   - "I feel annoyed."
   - "I'm creating boredom for me now."
   - "I'm tying myself up in knots."

- "I turned my head."
- "I got myself fired up."
- "I gave myself a complex."

C. Begin your thought or sentence with, "I'm choosing."
- "I'm choosing annoyance."
- "I'm choosing boredom."
- "I'm choosing frustration."
- "I'm choosing unbridled excitement."
- "I'm choosing to brighten my day by thinking thoughts of her."

Prescription 3

Use the word "doing" in your language as you describe your feeling or behavior.

"I am doing depression."

"I am doing a broken heart right now."

"I'm doing sadness."

"I'm doing pure joy."

If Chick says to himself or to a friend, "Apparently, I'm doing depression right now," what's likely to follow is, "Why would I want to do that?" His answer to his own question would likely be, "I *don't* want to do depression." When you know you are doing depression and you want to change it, it's easier if you know you're in charge. It's much more difficult to stop doing depression if you think the economy, your evaluation, or the monthly sales report is doing it to you. Own it and you can end it more easily.

Prescription 4

Feel the feeling and know you are creating it. You don't have to change it if you choose not to. There is nothing wrong with feeling anger, frustration, anxiety, or any other emotion. It's OK to simply feel the feeling and move through it.

Sometimes fighting a feeling gives it more power and encourages it to hang around longer. Feel it and let it go. One day Thomas commented to his friend Edmundo, "You look tired." "No, I'm not tired," Edmundo responded. "I'm just doing depression." "How long do you think you'll keep doing that?" Thomas asked. "Not sure," Edmundo said. "I've decided not to fight it. I'm going to do it and do it really well. I want to really do it up right. I think I'll be able to let go of it faster that way."

Prescription 5

Use "ing" more often.

"I'm depress*ing* myself with worry."

"I'm bor*ing* myself."

"I'm bad mood*ing* right now."

"I'm turn*ing* myself on with thoughts of her."

"I'm anxiet*ing*."

Our prediction is that your next comment is likely to be . . . Are you ready? Here it comes . . . *"That doesn't sound right. People don't talk that way. It's not normal. No one ever says, 'I'm depressing myself.' It sounds weird."*

You're right. Most people don't talk that way. The overwhelming majority of people communicating on planet Earth today speak with unself-responsible, dis-ease-infected language. When they use that style of speaking, they perpetuate sickness by innocently spreading it worldwide.

Self-responsible language is indeed a foreign language to most of us. Did you ever attempt to learn a foreign language? Our guess is that it sounded funny at first. Perhaps even weird for a while. Then, as you continued to work with the new language and became familiar with it, it seemed more normal to your ear. The same concept holds here and can be helped by implementing prescription 6.

Prescription 6

Practice. Practice. And practice some more. Healthy language could sound awkward at first. Many of us are not used to hearing people talk self-responsibly or talking that way ourselves. It could sound like a new psychological technique, a recently invented form of manipulation, or just plain unusual.

Keep on talking, using healthy, dis-ease-free language. Eventually it will begin to sound normal, and it will then be your old way of speaking that will sound weird.

Imagine a conversation a few months from now.

"How did the game go last night?"

"It went well until I started thinking anxiously."

"What do you mean?"

"I was pitching well, got four outs in a row, and didn't walk anyone. Then I remembered this is the best-hitting team in our league, the first-place team. I started thinking about the last time we played them, when I got hit pretty hard."

"And . . . ?"

"I started doing anxiety, forgot to focus, and walked three batters in a row."

"So thinking about last time made you nervous?"

"No, it was more like I created nervousness for myself by thinking unhelpful thoughts."

"Oh, so your nerves got to you."

"Not exactly. In reality, I began doing nervousness to myself."

"Why would you want to do that?"

"That's the same question I asked myself. I decided I didn't want to create nervousness, so I stopped thinking about the last time and focused on the challenge of this time."

"You did that while you were on the mound?"

"Yes, and between innings when we were batting. I changed my thoughts. I said to myself, 'This isn't nervousness. It's excitement.' So I focused on the excitement of pitching and pictured myself putting the ball right where I wanted it to go."

"What happened?"

"I did a lot better. No more walks, and I stopped doing anxiety."

"Who won?"

"They did."

"So this 'positive thinking' thing really didn't work."

"I don't call it positive thinking, although it is certainly positive. I call it managing my own mind to produce a desired result."

"Well, it didn't work."

"Yes, it did."

"You said you got beat."

"Yep. They scored more runs than we did. And I succeeded in managing my own mind. I produced the result I wanted."

"Losing?"

"I didn't have total control over whether we won or lost. I did have control over how I managed my mind. I stopped creating anxiety and began doing excitement instead. I succeeded in that, pitched a lot better, and gave my team an opportunity to win. We lost in the last inning on an error by our shortstop."

"Bet that made you mad."

"No, I chose to be empathetic. Anger didn't seem like a healthy choice at that point."

"Man, you're talking funny. Have you been to one of those workshops again?"

"Actually, I have. I made a decision to attend a full- day seminar on the Abracadabra Effect. The presenters talked about 13 verbally transmitted diseases and how to cure them."

"Well, they've got you talking funny."

"I'm glad you noticed. I believe I have indeed chosen to talk differently since that experience."

"What made you do it?"

"Nothing 'made me.' I simply decided I wanted to take more self-responsibility in my life because . . . "

"Hey, I've got to go. My kids are going to be ticked off if I don't pick them up on time."

"They choose to get upset if you're not right on time?"

"It makes them mad."

"They choose anger?"

"Well, it's not a choice really. It just comes over them."

"Like an angry cloud that covers them and drips anger?"

"Something like that. Hey, gotta go."

The Cure

So far, we've concentrated on prescriptions designed to treat the symptoms. What would it take to create a cure? What would elimination of the "Makes Me" Psychosis look like? The answers to those questions are coming up in the next chapter.

Chapter 4
Into the Future

You can lead a horse to water, but you can't make him drink.

The sentence above includes the correct use of "makes me." It is an accurate statement. You cannot make a horse drink water.

Imagine a world where "makes me" and similar language constructions were only used correctly. What if all the "makes me" variations described in the previous pages were eliminated from our language patterns? What if no one talked that way? What if no one believed that another person could make them mad? What would that world look like?

"*Stop. Hold it right there,*" you might be thinking. "*Now you're going to give us the cure for something that isn't all that much of a problem. 'Makes me' is no big deal. I don't see the problem.*"

You don't see a problem? You don't see any dysfunction, nor any dis-ease embedded in "makes me" language? Maybe this will help. Let's take a look at one of your possible lives, delivered here in language bursts from beginning to end. See what you think.

"Not getting chocolate ice cream makes me mad."

"My new baby brother is annoying."

"Forcing me to eat vegetables makes me pout."

"My parents irritate me."

"School bores me."

"My boyfriend lights up my life."

"The coach fires me up."

"Being accepted at the university makes me excited."

"Algebra frustrates me."

"The guy sitting next to me in U.S. History turns me on."

"I lost my virginity the night he swept me off my feet."

"Tests stress me out."

"Graduation brings relief."

"The new job excites the heck out of me."

"Getting engaged makes me happy."

"My fiancée completes me."

"Getting married thrills me."

"Getting pregnant uplifts me."

"The thought of oral sex turns me off."

"Our financial condition worries me."

"My new little girl is my sunshine."

"My husband getting laid off depresses me."

"Having my husband around all the time is annoying."

"Vacation relaxes me."

"My two kids are driving me up a wall."

"My children's teachers make me happy."

"My teenager fell in with the wrong crowd."

"My husband's request for a divorce infuriates me."

"Now, he's not sure. He keeps me hanging on."

"Late child support checks make me furious."

"I got carried away with the credit cards."

"Dating again makes me nervous."

"Being a grandma makes me feel old."

"Where did my life go? Time just got away from me."

"The thought of dying scares me."

"The devil made me do it."

Congratulations, you just managed to ignore reality and live an unself-responsible, unconscious life from beginning to end. *Abracadabra.* You get to do that if you want. Lots of people make that choice. On the other hand, you could choose self-responsible, reality-based, dis-ease- free living. That choice would require self-responsible language patterns, self-responsible thinking, self-responsible beliefs, and self-responsible behaviors. Lots of people make that choice, also. *Abracadabra* again.

Imagine a time in the future. Imagine a culture where "makes me" language is not used, where it is unknown, where all the strands of "makes me" are simply missing. Can you imagine what that would be like?

"*Hold on again.*"

"What do you mean 'hold on'? Are you choosing to interrupt this imagine-the-future section again?"

"Yep. Here's why. These language patterns that you think are so terrible are simply idioms. No one really believes you light my fire, he steered me the wrong way, or my children pushed my buttons. We all know no physical rubbing occurred when she said he rubbed her the wrong way. Everyone knows there was no rope involved when someone says a movie tied them up in knots. These are merely innocent phrases, nothing more that conversational habits. So stop bugging me."

When you say, "Stop bugging me," we agree that you're using an idiom and there are no actual bugs present. What we do not agree with is that this is an innocent, harmless, benign phrase. It is not benign. It is filled with dis-ease of the "you make me" variety.

Agreed, there was no rope, no hands that rubbed, no actual button that got pushed, and no one grabbed your head and physically turned it. But ALL of these, what you label "innocent phrases," are not so innocent. Every one of them carries the false message that someone can "make me" feel, behave, speak, or respond in a certain way. Every one of these phrases is packaged with the message that you are not in control of your responses to life. Each one points down a road that leads to giving up your personal power and weakening your self-responsible-language immune system, leaving you more susceptible to the "Makes Me" Psychosis.

When we use this style of articulation, we reinforce our false belief that a situation or person can *make us* do or feel something. As a result of thousands of repetitions of "makes me" language, we now live in a culture where self-responsible thinking and behaving are endangered species. Yes, these idioms are conversational habits. They are conversational habits that are destructive to our emotional and mental health. They are conversational habits that can be replaced with self-empowering ones that leave us in a state of health and linguistic wellness.

Now back to the chapter . . .

Imagine a time in the future. Imagine a culture where "makes me" language is not used, where it is unknown, where all the strands of "makes me" are simply missing. Can you imagine what it would be like?

From birth on, children would only hear self-responsible language and language patterns as detailed in the following chapters. Since they never heard "makes me" or any of its insidious variations, they would have no concept of anyone "making them," pushing their buttons, depressing them, annoying them, or of being overtaken by a mood. They would develop no belief system that included the notion that they had the power to "make" someone mad, frustrate them, or drive them crazy. Those notions would be foreign to them, as foreign as any language that was not present and filling their ears in their early years.

"*Wait a minute. Sorry to interrupt again and break your train of thought, but I just thought of something. My responses happen so quickly I don't have time to decide how I want to interpret them. I still think a deer that runs in front of my car on my drive home makes me frightened. It's like a conditioned response. The fear happens so quickly. I don't have time to think about it. What do you have to say about that?*"

You might choose to be surprised by our response. The first part of our answer is that you're correct. Perhaps there is a physical fight-or-flight response that just happens so quickly we aren't able to choose our interpretation. Physiologically, our body responds to events that occur around us. A large portion of that response takes place in our autonomic or automatic nervous system.

Think back to high school biology for a moment. Most of us are familiar with sympathetic activation. That's what is commonly known as the "fight or flight" response. When the fight-or-flight system is triggered, hundreds of chemicals flood into the body within milliseconds. These chemicals prepare us to handle the situation by being ready to fight or to run. This is something that happens before we even think about it.

That fright, built into human beings over generations of life for survival, only lasts three or four seconds. Anything after that initial response is you keeping it going with your interpretive mind.

You might also choose to be surprised by the second part of our answer. This "automatic" response may not be so automatic after all. These responses can actually be regulated, controlled, and even altered. As a certified biofeedback technician, Thomas regularly works with individuals who have anxiety disorders and stress-related conditions. Using biofeedback, he teaches them how to self-regulate and control the autonomic nervous system responses that occur in relation to the events they are exposed to. The response is then based on the language the person uses and what he or she thinks and believes about the event.

Let's say you're leaving for work in the morning. You open the door and are confronted with a snarling Doberman. Your autonomic nervous system is activated. You can choose to scream and run or to speak calmly and perceive the dog as lost and in need of help. What you say to yourself in your interpretive mind will determine your response.

And just to keep the record straight, we want you to know we heard the words you used when you interrupted:

"*Sorry to interrupt again and break your train of thought.*"

No, you cannot break our train of thought. We are the only ones who can do that to ourselves. And so we resume . . .

Imagine a time in the future. Imagine a culture where "makes me" language is not used, where it is unknown, where all the strands of "makes me" are simply missing. Can you imagine what that would be like?

When generations of children have been raised to talk and think correctly, in sync with reality, this dis-ease will be no more. No one will be able to *make* people feel guilty, jealous, or frustrated. Individuals may choose some of those feelings, but they will be aware they are doing it to themselves. Incidents of anxiety, depression, and fear will be greatly reduced.

People will begin thinking and behaving more self-responsibly. Personal power will increase. Problems will get solved. Manipulation will become obsolete. Mental, emotional, and physical health will abound. Joy, happiness, love, and cooperation will flourish, and reality will reign. We will be cured of the "Makes Me" Psychosis!

Eliminating "makes me" statements is only the first of many ways you can change your language to change your life. In the chapters that follow we will detail more ways we use language to rob ourselves of joy, harmony, well-being, self-esteem, personal power, and self-responsible living. We will define additional verbal dis-eases and ways to inoculate yourself against their effects.

Is it time to take control of your language patterns and your life? Is it time to become the person you want to be? Is it time to move on to another of the 13 verbally transmitted diseases and how to cure them?

Chapter 5
Unableism

"Argue for your limitations and sure enough, they are yours."
—Jonathan Livingston Seagull

"I can't sing very well."
"It's too hot to mow the grass."
"I don't have a college degree."
"It's no use."
"That plan will be difficult to implement."
"I always have trouble closing the deal with her."
"I'm a morning person."
"I'm not mechanically inclined."
"I'm not what I used to be."
"I enjoy working for him, but it's tough sometimes."
"We don't have enough time."
"We'll never get it done."

The language examples on the previous page are ripe with infection. These dis-ease carriers contain viruses that may be preventing you from creating a life full of excitement, joy, trust, adventure, and possibility. They effectively limit your view of alternatives, exclude vast ranges of options, and discourage personal expansion. In short, they limit. We call this malady the language of "Unableism."

Unableism defined: The repetitious use of language that creates unnecessary boundaries that leave you feeling inadequate and incapable. A method for programming your mind with doubt and beliefs about yourself as being not enough. A method for effectively shutting off your personal power.

The predominant self-limiting phrase in our culture today is "I can't." You hear it often, frequently delivered with a whiny tone.

"I can't dance."

"I can't pass up double-dipped chocolate-covered peanuts."

"I couldn't help myself."

"I can't play golf well."

"I can't quit smoking."

"I couldn't find it."

"I can't stop loving her."

None of the "I can't" statements above are true. Yes, you can dance. You are simply choosing not to at this time. You could play golf well. However, you aren't presently choosing to make the improvement of your golf game a priority in your life. Not passing up double-dipped chocolate-covered peanuts is not connected in any way to *can't*. It only reflects the decisions you make about how you are choosing to eat right now.

Most of our "I can'ts" are not true. When we use this limiting phrase, we dwell under the illusion that we are not responsible for the decisions we make. We get to pretend we don't have a choice. That choice of language eventually leads to beliefs and behaviors which distance us from taking responsibility. It absolves us of ownership of our attitudes or actions. By using it, we sabotage and weaken our perceived level of personal power. *Abracadabra.*

"I can't do it right now."

When you say, "I can't do it right now," you use language that implies no choice on your part. Actually, you *could* do it right now if you thought it was important enough. In reality, you might have a full day planned and you do not want to deviate from your plan. You could change your schedule. You could choose to do it right now. You are choosing not to.

Your "I can't" phrasing creates an image of yourself as a victim of circumstances, as someone who is out of control and powerless. That style of language keeps you from making a deliberate conscious choice and owning it. It is putting you at dis-ease.

"I can't quit smoking."

Why would you want to believe that about yourself? Of course you can quit smoking. But denying you have a choice is easier. It takes less effort. When you say, "I can't," you get to play victim. After all, it's not your fault. You just can't. You might think you're a victim when you say, "I can't." To us, it sounds more like a volunteer.

"I can't become a brain surgeon."

We could if we wanted to badly enough. So could you. We could become brain surgeons if we devoted most of our time and resources to achieving that goal. And we are choosing not to. Thomas is investing his energy in becoming a successful psychotherapist, husband, and father. Chick continues on his chosen path as a professional educator. Both of us are choosing to write and publish. So neither of us is interested in becoming a brain surgeon at this point in our lives. Still, neither of us is willing to say we can't. Why would we want to talk about ourselves as people who can't . . . anything? That would only serve to help us see ourselves as limited. We choose not to do that.

Remember that four-box schematic drawing we displayed earlier? You probably already suspect that "I can't" words lead to "I can't" thinking which results in "I can't" beliefs. And yes, most of our behaviors flow out of those beliefs. To simplify the connection demonstrated by the four boxes, let's just say your words are convincing you of something that is influencing your behaviors. Do you like what your words are telling you? Do you like what you have come to believe? Do you like the behaviors that result from using, thinking, and believing, "I can't?"

There is damage that results from the infection of Unableism language. There are strains of this dis-ease that are still left to be described here. There are warnings we intend to issue soon. And there are prescriptions you can implement to counter the language of Unableism, get healthy, and stay that way. But before we get to those important concepts, it's time to announce an important disclaimer.

Are you ready? Here comes the disclaimer. *Some "I can'ts" are real.* Yes, we actually said that. Some "I can'ts" are real. For instance, Thomas can't bear children without some kind of history-making surgery. Chick can't jump across the Pacific Ocean without the aid of some soon-to-be-invented jet propulsion backpack. Those are real "I can'ts" for us. You may have some that are real for you as well. However, before you create and experience the relief that comes along with putting some of your "I can'ts" in the mine-are-real category, we want to point out something important.

Did you notice that with our real "I can'ts" we qualified them? Thomas can't bear children *without some kind of history-making surgery.* Chick can't jump across the Pacific Ocean *without the aid of a jet propulsion backpack.* We are both hesitant to say "can't" about anything in our lives because that word abruptly slams the door on possibility. Why would we limit ourselves that way? We don't.

Before you decide whether one of your "I can'ts" is real or not, run it through the alternative language accuracy test below. Pick three or four "I can'ts." You can choose from the list below or create some of your own.

"I can't sing."

"I can't cook."

"I can't get the report in on time."

"I can't get organized."

"I can't stand the sales department."

"I can't get my teen to come home on time."

"I can't decide which one of the applicants to hire."

"I can't spell well."

"I can't get all the laundry done."

"I can't balance the budget."

"I can't think of any."

Now, using your "I can'ts," run them through the accuracy test. Say your "I can't" statements aloud using the following four sentence starters. Pause and reflect on how your statements sound after each starter. Pay attention to your internal reaction and self-talk as you listen to them and reflect on what you hear and feel.

1. I can't . . .
2. I don't . . .
3. I won't . . .
4. I choose not to . . .

We'll use "I can't get all the laundry done," "I can't golf well," and "I can't cook" as examples. Using the sentence starters provided, the statements would be as follows:

Example one:

"I can't get all the laundry done."

"I don't get all the laundry done."

"I won't get all the laundry done."

"I choose not to get all the laundry done."

Example two:

"I can't golf well."

"I don't golf well."

"I won't golf well."

"I choose not to golf well."

Example three:

"I can't cook."

"I don't cook."

"I won't cook."

"I choose not to cook."

Get in touch with your internal reactions to saying your statements with the suggested sentence starters. Much like a thermometer a doctor uses to determine your temperature, your reactions will give you useful information to determine your degree of infliction with Unableism.

When you used "don't," did it help you become aware of the part you play in not cooking or getting the laundry done? Did it leave you feeling more personally empowered and in control? Did it seem inaccurate for your statements? You get to decide.

When you used, "I won't play golf well," did it seem final? Did it have a stubborn ring to it? Did you experience a sense of relief, as if you had already made a firm decision about the issue? Did it sound negative or positive? Did you become determined to work to change it?

How did "choose not to" sound to you? Did you enjoy it because it helped you see the choices you are making in your life concerning your perceived "I can'ts"? Or did you become defensive and justify the self-limiting language? Do you still choose to believe you are not responsible for your "I can'ts"?

Some people who do this exercise are uncomfortable feeling responsible. They prefer saying, "I can't," to examining how they might be creating their own limits. Others feel guilt when they conclude they are responsible for the state of their "I can'ts." Still others seem relieved and empowered as they move their "I can'ts" through the accuracy test.

Whatever your reaction to the exercise above, we defend your right to have it and keep it. You can think and believe whatever you choose about the activity and your reactions to it. If you want to cling to your "I can'ts," for whatever reason, you can have them.

If you believe and articulate, "I can't sing," here is your payoff. You get to be right. You get to not sing. If you believe, "I can't cook," again you get to be right. You get to not cook. In addition to being right, you earn an added bonus. You get to reduce your personal power and feelings of competency by functioning with the debilitating condition of Unableism and imposing imaginary limits on yourself. *Abracadabra.*

Combining Illnesses

We recently received a Facebook status that announced, "Somebody got me started playing Candy Crush and now I can't stop." This is a perfect example of layering one level of sickness on top of another. "Somebody got me started" is blatant self-infliction with the "Makes Me" Psychosis (chapter 2). "And now I can't stop" doubles down on illness by adding Unableism to the mix. "I chose to get started playing Candy Crush and am choosing not to stop for now" claims ownership of your choices and puts personal back in your control. It's a healthier way of speaking.

Harmful Effects

Imagine the following situation. Rebecca and Olivia are both preparing for an important job interview. Because they both want to create a favorable first impression, they're preparing to dress for success. New spring suits have just arrived at an upscale clothing store. They're both expecting to shop and purchase.

Also imagine that Rebecca and Olivia have a similar financial situation. Their financial status and ability to pay are identical. Both of their purses are filled with an equivalent amount of cash. Their desire for the job and their desire for a new spring suit are equal. They even want the same suit.

Rebecca notices the suit, tries in on, and loves it. She looks at the price tag and remarks, "I can't afford it." Later in the day, Olivia notices the suit, tries it on, and says, "I choose not to buy it." Both walk out of the store without the suit.

Same situation. Same desire. Same ability to pay. Same decision. Both leave without the suit. So what's different? Their words. And because their words are different, the pictures they create of themselves and the beliefs those words reinforce are different.

Rebecca, who says, "I can't afford it," is choosing a style of language that creates a picture of herself as a person without enough money. She is setting herself up as limited and living in a state of lack. Her words focus on the concept of not enoughness. The message she sends herself is that she can't and has little choice.

Olivia made the same decision Rebecca did. Both left the store without the suit. Olivia, however, creates a much different picture of herself by the language she chooses to describe her decision. By saying, "I chose not to buy it," Olivia creates an image of herself as a person who is acting prudently; someone who has executed self-will and made a clear decision based on a desire for the suit tempered by other priorities. Also implied in Olivia's reaction is an attitude of abundance coupled with choice. ("I can afford it, and I choose not to buy it.")

Rebecca activated language patterns contaminated by Unableism and left the store with her head down, feeling poor, powerless, and without choice. Olivia, using healthy language, left the store with her head high, congratulating herself on making a wise decision, feeling abundant and powerful.

Prescriptions

So suppose you want to get well? What if you're tired of the self-limits that accompany your "I can't" language? Is there an antidote?

Yes, there are several exercises you can do to strengthen your "able" muscles and combat this dis-ease. First, when you become conscious of yourself saying, "I can't," stop. Use the accuracy testing phrases "I don't," "I won't," and "I choose not to." Often, one of those phrases will seem more real for you than "I can't."

Sometimes "I don't cook" will feel more accurate than "I can't cook." On another occasion, "I won't golf" may be the most accurate of the phrases. At times, "I choose not to get organized" will sound and feel the healthiest and most personally empowering. Go with whatever feels right to you at the time. In each case, you will be moving closer to a full recovery and optimum activation of your verbal immune system.

It doesn't have to follow.

Use the healing ointment "It doesn't have to follow." When you hear yourself saying, "I can't get to work on time," tag on "It doesn't have to follow." Rubbing that sentence into your aching attitude will provide temporary relief from your erroneous mindset. It will re-mind yourself that "can't" does not have to be your permanent reality. You can create a new reality if you choose.

Healthy sentence enders

Following are four healthy sentence enders you can use to reduce the duration and severity of Unableism.

"yet."

"so far."

"at this time."

"at this point."

When you hear yourself say, "I can't," aloud or to yourself, add one of these healthy sentence enders.

"I can't spell well *yet.*"

"I can't decide which one of the applicants to hire *at this point.*"

"I can't get all the laundry done *at this time.*"

"I can't balance the budget *so far.*"

We recommend you use these healthy sentence enders at the first sign of Unableism. They are safe to use in conjunction with other prescriptions listed in this section. Do not use with unexplained foot pain. If Unableism persists, do not consult a doctor. Immediately implement the following prescription.

Act as if, pretend, or play like.

When a symptom of Unableism appears, take action. Think you can't dance? Act as if you can. Believe you can't get your desk cleared off? Pretend you can. Hear yourself saying, "I can't stand the sales department"? Play like you can. Don't believe you can get rid of depression? Act as if you are not depressed. It's easier to act your way to a feeling than to feel your way to an action.

Don't think you believe anything in this chapter? Act as if you do. Watch what happens.

Chapter 6
"I Can't" Variations

Similar to "makes me," "I can't" also has a variety of mutations that are invading our language patterns and disturbing our overall wellness. Regardless of their disguise, all are clear examples of how people put themselves at dis-ease by imposing imaginary and often unrecognized limits on themselves.

Are you using language patterns to choke off possibility in your life? Do your words lead to thoughts and beliefs that create a stranglehold that binds and restricts you from living your fullest life? If your words limit choice, confine your thoughts, or prevent a full view of yourself as a responsible, empowered individual, you are unconsciously injuring yourself with dis-eased language patterns. Let's take a closer look.

"It's no use talking to her."

The statement above is true. If you really believe talking to her is of no use, then it's of no use for you.

The statement above is false. There is plenty of use in talking to her if you believe there is.

Either way, you get to be right.

What you believe about talking to her is what makes it true or false for you. How you choose to talk about the situation is what creates and reinforces your belief about it.

"I'm unable to . . ."

Marcia had two miscarriages within a nine-month period. Both were spontaneous abortions that she endured alone in the bathroom just off the master bedroom. Because of her internal reactions (trauma) to the experiences, she never attempted to have children again. For fifteen years following her miscarriages, Marcia lived her life in emotional pain. Discomfort and dis-ease filled her days from that time on.

After much pleading from her husband, Marcia finally entered therapy. During her first therapy session Marcia exclaimed, "I'm *unable* to be happy. I lost everything in that bathroom and *I can't* get over it. That *bathroom has robbed me* to this day."

If you have read this far, you probably know it was not the bathroom that robbed Marcia. It was her internal interpretation of the events and her personal reaction to them. On some level, she has been unconsciously robbing herself of joy, peace, and healthy living.

It is our hope that Marcia will continue in therapy and thoroughly explore and experience the grieving process. We believe she will eventually rid herself of the words she used to create dis-ease in herself and establish a new set of thoughts and beliefs to carry her forward toward full health.

"I'd like to be able to . . ."

"I'd like to be able to learn a foreign language."

"I'd like to be able to tell my supervisor I think she's making a mistake."

"I'd like to be able to finish my master's degree."

"I'd like to be able to stop saying, 'He made me mad.'"

"I'd like to be able to" is nothing more than a sugar-coated substitute for "I can't." Under that sugar exterior lies a bitter pill that you think helps you feel better because it contains elements of "I want to, but." Do not be deceived. "I'd like to be able to" is as harmful as "I can't" in its purest form. Many people unknowingly use it to limp through their lives wrapped tightly in their own self-inflicted bondage. They create their own hitch in their own step and are not aware they have done it to themselves.

"I always . . ." and "I never . . ."

"I *always* miss a sale with him."

"I *never* win contests."

"We *never* play well against them."

"I *always* have trouble getting started."

How do you use "always" and "never"? Do you use them to close down options or to increase the range of possibilities in your life? If you use them in ways similar to those listed above, you clog the healthy flow of your natural life force. In the first example, your language positions you beyond just missing a sale with him now. You have created yourself as *always* missing a sale with him. If you missed getting a sale with him, you missed getting a sale with him. There is no need to add an element of finality to it by using "always."

Use "always" and "never" for your own advantage. Use them in ways that serve you. Lay a foundation for your belief system to grow in a healthy, nonrestrictive way. Use language that makes room for increased possibility and personal power in your life.

"I *always* give people more than their money's worth."

"My mind *always* produces several creative ideas each day."

"I *never* slow up when I near the end."

"I *always* get another opportunity to create a sale with him" will add more jump and vitality to your next step. Give yourself a shot of health.

Negative Predictions

"I probably won't interview well."

Not if you talk and think like that you won't. Why predict failure? Why use language that fosters negative anticipation? Plant seeds of success with, "I'll knock this interview out of the park."

"These directions are complicated."

"This is going to be difficult."

Are you sure you want to believe it's going to be difficult? You can change your mind and your forecast by changing your words. If you have yourself severely locked into the belief that the directions are complicated and feel the urge to say, "But they *really are* complicated," then at least add a qualifier to your statement. "I am currently choosing to perceive the directions as being complicated, so it's a good thing I'm persistent and don't give up easily." Start eliminating your self-imposed chains one link at a time.

"This could be tough."

Yes, it could be tough. It could also be easy, fun, exciting, challenging, simple, stimulating, entertaining, thrilling, boring, dull, or exhilarating. You get to have it your way. Just stay conscious that you are indeed the creator of this reality. *Abracadabra.*

"It isn't easy."

"It isn't easy to pass up chocolate cake." Now why would anyone want to believe that? If you believe it won't be easy, then it won't be easy for you. So here we go again with another example of someone inflicting himself with limiting words, thoughts, and beliefs that make it more difficult for him to powerfully handle situations that appear in his life.

"That's impossible."
"My coworker is impossible to work with."

You know what we're going to say here, so please consider saving us all some time and space and simply say it to yourself. The best mental floss is the kind you administer to yourself anyway.

"I am . . ."

Two of the most important words in the English language are "I am," along with the words that follow them. These words firmly cement erroneous beliefs in our consciousness. They invite us to identify with the condition that follows them.

"I am nervous."

"I am tired."

"I am sick."

"I am exhausted."

If you say, "I am tired," you identify with tired. The more you talk about it, the more you feel it and the more firmly you cement it into your biocomputer's belief system.

Concentrate on illness and you feel more ill. If you are sick, stop feeding it energy. Stop talking about it. Stop strengthening it in your consciousness. Refuse to identify with it. Talk about health and choose words that talk about improvement. Your friends, your relatives, and your illness will welcome the change.

Feeling old? Stop talking about it. Stop thinking about it.

"I'm not what I used to be."

"It must be my age."

"I'll be forty next month. I don't even want to think about it."

"I have AAADD, Age Activated Attention Deficit Disorder."

"My memory is not what it used to be."

Chick's professional speaking opportunities have been dropping slowly over the past several years due in part to the economy and cutbacks in money for schools and staff development. This has happened at the same time that he's beginning to move into semiretirement mode. Recently he heard himself tell friends, "I'm slowing down. My body is slowing down. My business is slowing down, and it's all OK. It seems like divine timing, the perfect time to slow down."

Did you notice what he was telling himself? So did Chick. And he didn't like how it sounded. So he changed his words and stopped feeding the belief system that he's slowing down. If you ask him now if he's slowing down, Chick will tell you, "No way. I'm busy reinventing myself." He is moving rapidly toward generating different income opportunities, including assisting with the writing and marketing of this manuscript. And yes, he is moving forthrightly toward semiretirement and all the exciting activities he's creating with that. Slowing down? Not a chance.

Harmful Effects

High doses of the language of Unableism result in weakened resolve to take charge of your own life and decreased response-ability. This dis-ease weakens your personal power immune system and leaves you susceptible to a diminished belief in yourself and your abilities. Accomplishment, energy, joy, excitement, closure, adventure, and satisfaction are likely to suffer as a result. If left untreated, a rapid decline in personal power is likely to follow.

Your language can imprison or free you. Characterized by high amounts of doubt and illusion, Unableism takes root in your thoughts, spreads to your beliefs, and builds boundaries that often go undetected. Once in place, these boundaries exclude, discourage, and subtract possibilities from your life.

"Can't," "difficult," "never," "always," and "I am" followed by a negative attribute are verbally transmitting Unableism into your being and may be preventing you from experiencing a life full of choice, rich with healthful benefits and exciting possibilities.

Prescription 1: Pay attention.

Listen to yourself. What do you hear yourself saying? Your words are convincing you of something. Do you like what they're telling you? If not, you can limit your own limiters by choosing words that reveal alternatives and possibilities. You can self-medicate with the language of possibility.

To eliminate outdated thinking that triggers the dynamic of Unableism it's important to stay conscious of your self-talk. When you notice unhealthy language, stop. Immediately reconstruct your words and your thoughts.

How are you reacting to the last two paragraphs? Are you telling yourself it will be difficult? If so, start now to heal yourself of this language sickness. Begin the process of rubbing healing salve on yourself by changing your words in this present moment.

Prescription 2: Change trains.

We've heard it said that the greatest transportation system in the world is your train of thought. We endorse that concept. The place where you find yourself in your life right now is a direct result of the thoughts you have amassed up to this point. That collection of thought has brought you to this destination. Likewise, the thoughts you are currently thinking are leading you in a direction that leads to a future destination. Do you like where your present thought is leading? If not, change trains.

Prescription 3: Exercise.

A single dose of changing your language will most likely not eradicate several years' worth of abusing yourself with unhealthy language. A sustained effort of regularly exercising your new language muscles will help you build the strength necessary to combat this dilapidating illness. Vigor will return to your language and your life if you practice replacing language patterns regularly. Get out there and get moving.

Prescription 4: Burn, bury or flush.

A dramatic demonstration will often help kick-start the medicine contained in the prescriptions listed above.

Write your unabling language examples on file cards. Read them through one more time. Then take them to a burn pile, light them on fire, and watch them go up in smoke. Visualize the Unableism leaving your body and rising into the air and out into the universe. Feel the freedom that accompanies releasing this dis-ease agent's grip on you.

Or dig a "grave" on your property and bury your file cards. Know they will rest in peace. Honor the dead language patterns with a prayer and mark the spot. Every time you pass the grave site, smile and give thanks for your growing long-term benefits.

Another possibility is to write your examples on toilet paper and flush them. Send them down the toilet, where they belong with the other excrement.

Possible Side Effects

Implementing these prescriptions may result in serious side effects, including strange looks from friends, questions about what has happened to you, and efforts to convince you you're out of your mind. It may produce comments such as, "You can't do that," and, "It'll never happen," from coworkers and friends. If these side effects continue or worsen, find some new friends and coworkers.

Chapter 7
Preventarrhea

Bumper sticker seen on a car in Columbus, Ohio:
Nothing Is Too Anything.

"It's too cold."
"It's too hot."
"It's too expensive."
"It's too cheap."
"It's too nice."
"I'm too slow."
"I'm too fast."
"I'm too frightened."
"I'm too young."
"I'm too old."
"It takes too long."

"That's too much."

"It's too hard."

"She's having too much fun."

Marietta Jenklins was the tenth caller to a local radio station recently. Informed that she had won a one hundred dollar gas certificate for her timely call, she announced to all the listeners, "I don't believe it. It's too good to be true."

When Watson Letharty was encouraged by his father to consider becoming a softball umpire for the local recreation department, he quickly replied, "I don't have enough experience. I'm too young."

"That's too complicated for me" were the words uttered by Tevi McCarty when asked by his coworker for some help cleaning up her computer.

All these examples point to an overly enthusiastic and excessive use of the word "too." This verbal hyperactivity invades the mind, disorients our thinking, and dramatically affects our behavioral choices. Overuse of "too" creates dis-ease and has become the premier verbal preventer in the English language. It is a verbal signal that "Preventarrhea" is present.

Preventarrhea defined: The use of language to delay, omit or quit an activity without taking responsibility or ownership for the choice. A primary preventer to help you stay unconscious while procrastinating or giving up.

People use "too" to prevent taking action and following through.

"It's too hot to mow the grass."

"It's too late to begin this project."

"It's too wet to go outside and exercise."

People use "too" to prevent seeing themselves as able.

"I'm too sad to move off the couch."

"I have too many expenses to save for retirement now."

"My feet are too tired to walk that far."

People use "too" to prevent taking full responsibility for the way they act.

"I'm too mad to apologize to her."

"I'm too frustrated to make it work."

"I was too nervous to stop eating."

People use "too" to prevent risk or change.

"I'm too old to start looking for a new job."

"She's too busy to answer my question."

"I've gone too far to ask for a divorce now."

People use "too" after the fact as an excuse to justify actions or inaction.

"I was too distracted to notice."

"It was just too late to begin a project that big."

"I was too nervous to make a strong presentation."

People use "too" to rationalize a result.

"It was too small of a booth to make many sales."

"It was too cold for me to get warmed up properly."

"She gave me way too much work for one person to complete in one day."

People use "too" to cop out.

"He was too upset with me so I didn't tell him."

"The drive was too long so we stayed home."

"The conference was too boring so I went shopping instead."

Have you noticed that even though "too" appears in a variety of situations for a number of different reasons, most of them are related to limits? Yes, Unableism is rearing its destructive head again and teaming up with Preventarrhea to produce a steady stream of dis-ease in our lives. The self-inflicted limits created with the use of "too" narrow our thinking and severely constrict our range of behavioral choices. That phenomenon results in opportunities lost, experiences missed, lessons unlearned, and potential joy left unrealized.

Prescription 1: Take the truth test.

Most varieties of "too" are not true. The temperature may by below zero. Still it is not too cold to get warmed up properly. It might take you longer to get thoroughly warmed up. You might have to do more stretching and go through your warm-up routine more than once. And it is NOT too cold to get thoroughly warmed up.

Is it really too late at night to finish that report? What if you could double your salary by finishing it tonight? Is it still too late?

Prescription 2: Own it.

We use evaluations during and after our seminars to collect data that will help us improve our participants' experience in the future. Recently we read one evaluative comment designed to give us information about the room temperature. "It's too hot in here" the workshop participant offered. The very next evaluation we read contained this feedback: "It was too cold in the room this afternoon."

So here is our feedback about that feedback. If you want to experience personal power in your life, own it. *It's* not too hot or too cold. *You* were colder or hotter than you would like to be. "I was cold this afternoon" or "I was experiencing the room as cold this afternoon" are self-responsible, empowering ways to speak. Leave "too" out of it.

Prescription 2: Push the delete button.

Once again, awareness is the key. When you become aware that you have used "too," an effective antidote is to repeat the sentence without it. Use the delete button on "too" and start over. Then add the healing ointment of an additional phrase that describes your choice.

"I'm too frustrated to make it work" now becomes "I'm frustrated and I choose to take a break from fixing it right now." "My feet are too tired to walk that far" can be altered to become, "My feet are tired and I choose not to walk that distance." "I have too many expenses to save for retirement" can be reformed to communicate to yourself and others, "I have expenses and I choose (or choose not) to save for retirement."

Whether you choose to save or not save for retirement in this moment is not the issue. Nor is it your deciding to walk to the bank or not. The real issue is: Are you speaking in a way that expands your awareness of the possibilities that exist? Or are you preserving the illusion of powerlessness by verbally disguising the decisions you make from yourself, placing the responsibility for those choices on conditions being "too" something? *Abracadabra.*

Chapter 8
Preventarrhea Continued

Get off your but to get off your butt!

"I'd like to make the report longer *but* I don't have time."

"I want to go to the Arabian horse show in Scottsdale, Arizona, this year *but* I don't have enough money."

"I want a promotion *but* I don't have the necessary skills."

OK, you read the word "but" in each of the sentences above. You're familiar with it. You've been hearing it and using it in sentences since before you were five years old. You probably started saying it before you realized the danger it represented to your mental and emotional well-being. No doubt you had no clue you were being quietly and regularly infected with a special strand of Preventarrhea. Likewise, you didn't realize you were activating the Abracadabra Effect.

"But" appears harmless enough at first glance. It would be easy to miss its significance. It's such a tiny word. It contains only three letters. How could it possibly be compromising our immune systems and facilitating the spread of Preventarrhea? Let's put "but" under the microscope and take a closer look.

Have you got your mental microscope out and operating? If so, let's proceed. "But" is designed to be a connector that creates contrast between two parts of a sentence. How would that be limiting? How could that create dis-ease? How could that breed Preventarrhea? To find out, place the following slides under your microscope lens one at a time.

Slide #1: "I want a promotion *but* I don't have the necessary skills."

Look closely. Can you see through your microscope lens how "but" divides and builds distance between the two parts of the sentence? Do you see it? "I want a promotion," the first part of this sentence, and "I don't have the necessary skills," the second half of the sentence, are being driven apart by "but."

The use of "but" promotes either/or thinking. With "but" we tend to perceive the situation as one way or the other. When we believe the two parts of the sentence are mutually exclusive, we tend to act as if they are mutually exclusive. Because it comes last, what follows "but" often appears strongest, and we use it to prevent ourselves from taking positive action.

Slide #2: "I want to go to the Arabian horse show in Scottsdale, Arizona, this year *but* I don't have enough money."

Focus only on the first part of this sentence: "I want to go to the Arabian horse show in Scottsdale, Arizona, this year." When you talk like that, you sound powerful. Excitement is in the air. Possibilities abound.

Now focus on the second part of that sentence: "but I don't have enough money." Can you see your personal power being diluted right before your eyes? Watch as your desired trip changes from possible to improbable. Yes, "but" is a tiny word—and a powerful one. It's almost—shall we say it?—like magic.

Prescription 1

If you're serious about getting off your butt and accessing more personal power in your life, it will be helpful to get off your "but." The antidote for this unique form of Preventarrhea is to swap one three-letter word for another. Change "but" to "and."

"I want to go to the Arabian horse show in Scottsdale, Arizona, this year *and* I don't have enough money."

"And" is a combining word. It joins ideas rather than separates them. "And" invites us to perceive the whole picture rather than isolated and limited parts. It helps us see beyond mutually exclusive components to a broader vision than the limits created by the either/or thinking encouraged by "but."

Read the following sentences aloud as you keep your microscopes focused on the words and the feelings that result.

1. "I want to apply for the job *but* I am nervous."
2. "I want to apply for the job *and* I am nervous."

In each sentence the desire is strong and the expression of it sounds powerful. In example 1, "but" connects the wanting directly to a limiting factor which weakens the strength of the desire. "But" suggests restriction. Choices vanish. Personal power diminishes.

In example 2, "and" allows the wanting and the hindrance to stand side by side in the same sentence. This combination does not necessarily imply restriction. The desire is not diminished. It stays strong, allowing possibilities to flourish.

When you hear yourself saying, "I want to write a book but I don't know where to start," stop. Stop right there. Know that with the word "but" you are more likely to feel defeated. Stay conscious that your use of "but" will limit your vision of possibilities and weaken your sense of personal power. It will decrease the chance that you will ever write a book of any kind.

Change "but" to "and." Do it right now, right here, right away. Do it as soon as you hear the "but" come out of your mouth. No "buts" about it. Say, "I want to write a book *and* I don't know where to start." Your desire is still strong. Chances are you're going to begin looking around to see where to start. Guess what? You just started. You have now increased the likelihood that you will generate possibilities and take some form of positive action.

"Yeah, but . . ."

Yeah, but what?

Prescription 2

"I was going to, but . . ."

"I wish I could, but . . ."

"I was contemplating it, but . . ."

"I really wanted to, but . . ."

"I gave it my best effort, but . . ."

"I loved her, but . . ."

"I started to, but . . ."

"I know 'but' isn't healthy, but . . ."

"I don't want this to sound like an excuse, but . . ."

Guess what? It more than *sounds* like an excuse. It *is* an excuse.

Isn't it time you decided to kick some butt and eliminate the adverse effects of Preventarrhea? Isn't it time to butt out with the excuses and the dysfunction that results?

"*But* I'm just a morning person." In that case, read the next chapter first thing in the morning. Perhaps you will re-mind yourself of the impaired results that flow from that erroneous belief.

Chapter 9
Dead Enders as Preventarrhea

A devastating strand of Preventarrhea is currently operating in the world and may be at work in your life without your awareness or permission. Right now, it could be drastically limiting your ability to act by cutting off entire ranges of potential responses from your behavioral repertoire. If you have allowed it to invade your belief system, you have effectively denied yourself a multiple-option existence.

Choosing words in this category leave you with no way out. They limit both your vision and your choices. This style of verbal illness will propel you down a road that leads in only one direction, heading rapidly and unconsciously toward a dead end. This crippling version of Preventarrhea is so debilitating that we have given it a special name. We call this way of speaking "dead enders." Some examples follow.

> "That's just the way I am."
>
> "I'm just like my old man."
>
> "What do you expect from me? I'm a morning person."
>
> "I'm just a Pisces."
>
> "Hey, I'm Italian (Irish, Polish, Latin, Canadian, French, Southern, etc.) That's how we are."
>
> "I have a quick temper."
>
> "I'm a workaholic."
>
> "I'm too kind. I'm just a pushover."

All of the above are variations on the theme, "That's just the way I am." Each represents a self-imposed confinement from which there is no view of a way out. Each locks you into a cage of your own making that severely restricts your sense of personal power.

Take Mary Butler, for instance. Mary worked in the evening in a sleep study lab. She felt unfulfilled and insignificant as she hooked people to monitors and watched them sleep night after night. Yet she kept on doing it. Do you know why? As Mary put it, "I'm not a morning person. I just can't seem to get going fast enough in the morning to perform the way I think I should."

Teaching English to middle-school kids is what Mary really loved. Although she'd had a teaching degree for fifteen years, she didn't use it. In her words, "I don't see how I would ever be able to teach, being the 'night owl' I am."

Mary Butler, like a lot of people who use dead enders, limited her own response-ability. Because she said, "I'm just a morning a person," so often, she began to believe it. With repetitious use of those words, she convinced herself there were logical reasons why she continued to make the same limited and unsatisfying choices. Because she believed she wasn't a morning person, Mary noticed any evidence that proved to herself it was true. Mary's rational mind, not knowing it was infected with Preventarrhea, continued to generate messages that supported her disempowering belief. Hence, she stayed trapped in the dis-ease of being unfulfilled and thinking there was nothing she could do about it.

Feeling trapped and not knowing what to do, Mary entered counseling. Her counselor immediately recognized the dead-ender language and began helping her rescript and reframe it. As the dis-ease began to weaken, Mary took a few classes and studied for them in the evening at her sleep study job. Eventually, she obtained certification as a dyslexia specialist.

As Mary developed new language patterns, she began to challenge the dead-ender thinking that had led her down the path of limited response. She started working with kids in an after school program, teaching children with dyslexia how to read. She has since built up a reading recovery program, has left her job at the sleep study center, and currently teaches workshops for teachers. She works with students in the afternoon.

Mary still chooses to go slow in the morning and is now aware that is one of many options available to her. She has effectively expanded her range of possibilities. Mary is no longer feeling unfulfilled or stuck in a job she doesn't like.

If you continually argue that you behave the way you do because you are Italian or a Pisces or Southern, you are constricting your ability to respond outside of a stereotyped view of what that means.

If you regularly choose language that reinforces a belief that you have a quick temper or are a workaholic, you become blind to a variety of responses that demonstrate your ability to change your narrow and limiting self-definition. *Abracadabra.*

Go ahead and announce you are a chip off the old block, just like your dad, if you prefer. Be aware that when you do, you have narrowed your responses to a small set of choices that imitate your father's responses to life.

Do you really want to believe you're a pushover? When you continually use language that supports that belief, you provide fertile breeding ground for the harmful dis-ease Preventarrhea. You effectively prevent yourself from choosing more empowering ways to create and respect your own boundaries.

Following are more variations of "that's just the way I am."

"I'm not patient."

"I'm not creative."

"I'm all thumbs."

"I'm not mathematical."

"I'm uncoordinated."

"I'm not mechanical."

"I'm not religious."

"I'm easily angered."

"I'm just a typical woman (man)."

"I'm not musical."

"I'm a slow mover."

If you want to be a slow mover, keep telling yourself you're a slow mover. If your desire is to be easily angered, tell people, "I'm easily angered." If you really prefer to be uncoordinated, talk about it often to yourself and to others.

"But I really do function better in the morning," you might be thinking. Stop right there. You just violated the main notion of the previous chapter. Please repeat your statement again without the "but."

"I really do function better in the morning." OK, so what if that's true? What if you do function better in the morning? Are you 100 percent sure that's the case? Is it always true?

Do you function better in the morning because of your belief that you function better in the morning? Or do you believe you function better in the morning because you have noticed evidence that you function better in the morning?

Who cares? Regardless of your answer to this chicken-or-egg question, why would you ever want to say, "I am a morning person"? How does that serve you? How does it help you function more effectively throughout the day? How does that work for you when you have something important to accomplish at night?

Be careful what you tell yourself. You could be sending yourself down the dead end of severely curtailed response-ability. You might end up like Adrian.

Adrian was a hundred pounds overweight and diabetic. In addition to medication, her doctor recommended a regular exercise routine and a weight loss program. She agreed. After nearly two years of exercise and several diets, Adrian lost twenty pounds. She remains on medication and feels miserable. Sadly, Adrian continues to tell friends, "I don't know why I'm fighting this so hard. I can't change my body type. I'm big-boned. It's just the way I am." And so it is.

Prescription 1

Notice your dead enders. Healing this strand of Preventarrhea begins with the act of noticing. If you don't know a dead ender is present, there isn't much you can do to heal it.

If "That's just the way life is" goes unnoticed, you cannot alter its effects on your belief system. If "I have a quick temper" is not identified as a dead ender, you will continue to limit yourself with it unintentionally. If you don't hear yourself when you say, "I'm just a Pisces," you will be powerless to challenge that dis-eased statement.

Consciousness comes first. Becoming conscious of your language will help you recognize options in your life. Increased options means increased personal power. More options give you more power. Fewer options equal less power. Once you are aware of a dead ender, you have begun to claim your power. You can now choose to do something about it. Or not.

Challenge your one-way statements. Be ruthless in your examination of them. Yes, you are your mother's daughter. And do you do everything like her? All the time? Is "sensitive" really just the way you are? Or is sensitive how you chose to be the last five times? There is a difference.

Prescription 2

A useful way to respond when you notice yourself using a dead ender is to immediately swallow the "It doesn't have to follow" pill. That's right. Ingest that pill to negate dead enders the moment you hear yourself heading down that dead-end trail.

If you hear yourself say, "I'm a Smith. We're all like that," add, "It doesn't have to follow." That pill will help you remind yourself it doesn't have to be that way. There are other alternatives. More choices are available. Swallowing the "It doesn't have to follow" pill will, in time, eradicate the limiting effects of dead enders. You will now be more likely to examine many possibilities in a given situation.

Keep this important pill in the medicine cabinet of your mind. Take it on trips with you. Keep it within reach where you can access it quickly. If you hear yourself saying, "I'm not mechanical," self-medicate with "It doesn't have to follow."

Are you thinking these ideas are hard to remember? It doesn't have to follow.

Chapter 10
Shoulditus

Stop "shoulding" on yourself. And on others.

"I should mow the grass."

"I should clean the house."

"You should follow through immediately."

"I should exercise regularly."

"I should be working on that report right now."

"You should pay more attention to the sales department."

"You should read this chapter twice."

Shoulditus definition: A phrase designed to dispense guilt, shame, and blame on yourself and/or others. A method for getting after yourself so you will feel inadequate. A dis-ease that generates anxiety about what is yet to come or anger and frustration when others do not meet your expectations.

If you desire to put pressure on yourself and increase anxiety, use "should" and "ought to" regularly.

"I *ought to* send him a get well card."

"I *should* ask for a raise."

"I *ought to* tell him what I really think."

Use of "should" and "ought to" puts your focus on the difference between what exists now and what you feel "should" exist. It's a way to verbally apply negative pressure to yourself. This self-inflicted pressure increases the dis-ease produced by anxiety and stress. Shoulding on yourself sabotages your peaceful present moments, replacing them with frustration and guilt.

In addition to shoulding on ourselves, this dis-ease often takes the form of shoulding on others. Shoulding on others is an advice-dispensing mechanism that basically says, "I know better than you do." It's an effort to weaken the other person's power while increasing your own.

"You *should* call her right away."

"You *should* buy the truck."

"You *ought to* apologize to your employees immediately."

Most shoulds directed at others take the form of unasked-for advice. They flow from the belief, "I know better than you do what is best for you." This stance of superiority creates a big me/little you relationship that invites resistance and annoyance and creates distance. It comes from a judgmental, dis-eased mindset that believes others should be different from what they are at this moment.

"Should have" and "ought to have," another strand of Shoulditus, are verbal expressions that indicate you are playing out the role of a Monday morning quarterback. Whether directed at yourself or at others, you're looking to the past while attaching shame and fixing blame in the present.

"The advertising department *should have* listened to me."

"You *should have* asked me."

"They *ought to have* saved the money."

"We *shouldn't have* hired him."

"I *ought to have* warned her."

"Should have" or "shouldn't have" are not often recognized as a dis-ease because of the tendency to believe our "should haves" are accurate. It is clearly possible for you to make a strong case that someone "should have" or "shouldn't have" done something in a particular situation. You can gather an unlimited amount of "proof" that you are indeed correct. It's easy to make a case that someone should or should not have done something. So what?

What point is there to laying blame for what "should have" (in your mind) been done and wasn't? Where is that going to get you? Positive relationships are not built and maintained with shaming, blaming, or guilt tripping. Shoulding on another will not leave your spouse, child, boss, or coworker in an appropriate mood to search for solutions. When you should on them, you increase the chance they will choose the dysfunctional behavior of rigid defensiveness.

"Yes, but somebody should have noticed."

OK, let's say for the moment (purposefully ignoring your use of the word "but") that you're right.

The copywriters should have noticed.

The sales department should have noticed.

Your supervisors should have noticed.

The proofreaders should have noticed.

The mail room staff should have noticed.

The CEO should have noticed.

You should have noticed.

So assume for now we agree with you. Imagine we concur that the copywriters, the sales department, your supervisor, the proofreaders, the mail room staff, the CEO, and you "should have." Absolutely, someone should have. Guess what? No one did. And if they could have, they would have. They didn't.

It is not possible to redo present moments once they are no longer the present. Rewind is not available. It's time to move on. Any time invested lamenting how people used their present moments in the past is a waste of time. It keeps you stuck in the past and prevents you from taking corrective action now.

We're not suggesting you don't learn from the past. Certainly, examining what happened, learning from it, and taking corrective action are important. Go for it. All of that can be accomplished effectively without shoulding on one another.

Telling someone they "should have" works like a verbal grenade. When it blows up, both parties are injured and left to pick the shrapnel from their bruised feelings. Eliminate that weapon from your verbal arsenal and choose alternative ways of speaking described in the Shoulditis prescriptions below.

Prescription 1

The simplest way to eradicate Shoulditus is by replacing "should" with "could." Change "should haves" to "could haves."

"I *could* be working on that report right now" is less judgmental than "I *should* be working on that report right now."

"I *could* pay more attention to the sales department" is more descriptive than "I *should* pay more attention to the sales department."

"I *could* read this chapter twice" is less evaluative than "I *should* read this chapter twice."

"I *could* have warned her" is gentler than "I *should* have warned her."

"Could" is a word that describes the situation. It implies no evaluation. "I could pay more attention to the sales department" describes the situation. It tells what is possible in the here and now. Because "could" describes rather than judges, it makes the choices more visible. When you say, "I should be working on the report right now," you focus on yourself and get stuck in the evaluation. When you say, "I could be working on that report right now," you focus on the choice and recognize that working on the report or not is a decision.

Prescription 2

When you use "could," you give yourself an opportunity to make a decision. Personal power and personal responsibility dwell in decision making.

To heal Shoulditus, state your "could."

"I *could* call my mother."

"I *could* apply for the promotion."

"I *could* exercise regularly."

Decide whether or not you want to perform the behavior you stated you could right now. Are you going to call your mother or aren't you? "I could call my mother" doesn't mean you should. You get to decide with no shame or guilt attached. Just choose. Decide what you want and take action.

Once a decision is made, fear and anxiety diminish. Personal power and self-responsibility return. Dis-ease is replaced by ease.

Also examine the "could haves" you've used to replace "should haves."

"I *could have* told the truth."

"I *could have* bought the truck."

"I *could have* learned to speak Spanish when I was younger."

"I could haves" will help you focus on present options. Use them to decide what you want to do today. Using a double dose of "could" will help you determine what is best for you now.

"I *could* have learned Spanish when I was younger and I *could* take a Spanish class now." If you want to, go for it. If you don't want to, let that be OK.

"I *could* have told the truth and I *could* make amends and tell the truth from now on." You get to decide if you want to tell the truth or not. You could choose either option, without attaching any "shoulds" to it.

It's true you could have saved the money. You could have bought the truck rather than the jeep. You could have stayed late to finish the report. Certainly you *could* have. But *should* you have? That's up to you.

Possible Side Effects of Using This Medicine

You might end up like Gina and jettison people who have been regulators in your life.

Every day Gina's husband Rob would return home from his job as an engineer, ask Gina about her day, and then proceed to tell her what he thought she should have done differently. He thought he was being helpful. He wasn't.

The topic didn't seem to matter. According to Rob, Gina should have cooked spaghetti instead of baked chicken. She should have made the kids finish their homework before letting them go out to play. She should have taken the electric bill payment directly to the office instead of putting it in the mail. Rob consistently found something that, to his way of thinking, wasn't right. And he regularly let his wife know about it.

Rob is a master at what we commonly call "back-tracking." It's easy to look back over what someone else has done and find a flaw. What Rob fails to do is look at himself and see the damage he is causing in his relationship.

After several years of marriage, Gina sought legal advice. As she was explaining her situation to the attorney, he politely interrupted and said, "You should have left him sooner." Gina smiled, nodded her head, and immediately left the meeting. She began her search for a different attorney that same day.

The "medicine" outlined in this chapter is purposefully constructed to be used to protect yourself from accepting the disease of Shoulditus from other people. When your partner, supervisor, coworker, or relative informs you that you "should have" done something, take charge of how you hear it. You cannot control how it is said to you and you *can* control how you hear it. Hear shoulds and oughts as data. Train yourself to hear them as information others are sharing about their preferences. Consider the information they're offering you if you wish. Think about altering your behavior in the future if you choose.

Warning: People who have previously been successful at guilt tripping you may become suddenly irrational. The change in your response to their guilt tripping may trigger episodes of inappropriate language and manipulative behavior. Ignore them or create physical distance between you and them.

Advice givers may mysteriously disappear from your life. Do not chase after them.

This is not intended to be a complete list of all side effects that may occur. If you have questions about side effects, call a verbal skills professional at your earliest convenience.

Overdose Information

It is not possible to overdose with these prescriptions. Use them often and in abundance.

Chapter 11
Judgmentalillness

You see the title of this chapter: *Judgmentalillness*. How do you react? Are you judging it? Do you think it's stupid, clever, cute, or ridiculous? If so, you are manifesting dis-ease in your life right here, right now. You might not realize it. You might not agree. And you are definitely exhibiting a major symptom of Judgmentalillness.

Judgmentalillness definition: A language trap that limits vision and narrows perspective. A tendency to blame, criticize, and compare that hinders perception and signals the need to be right.

There is no escaping this common dis-ease. It is everywhere in our culture. It begins at birth. Within minutes of your appearance on earth you were judged as healthy, beautiful, cute, homely, ugly, strong, loud, happy, and so on. As a toddler, the judgment continued. You were constantly being evaluated:

when you walked and talked, how long you took naps, where and when you went potty, and how often you whined or smiled.

Then you went off to school and, thankfully, the judgment finally ended. No, it didn't. Incidents of Judgmentalillness intensified. You were tested and rated on your level of mastery on a narrow skill set that had little to do with real learning. You were placed in a reading group or given color-coded reading packets based on educators' judgments of your reading level. You were given external judgmental measures of your efforts, including stars, stickers, smiley or frowny faces, student of the week awards, public performance charts, grades, and red pencil markings. You were mentioned at award assemblies, made the honor roll, and qualified for the National Honor Society, or not. Parent/teacher conferences were held to communicate how you compared to other students using grade-level norms.

You now live in a society that is obsessed with rating, ranking, scoring, comparing, and attaching judgments to movies, basketball teams, meat, golfers, men and women, horses, cars, music, stocks, grapefruit, and more. Our language patterns abound with good and bad, skinny and fat, ugly and beautiful, awful and wonderful, lazy and ambitious, boring and exciting, and stupid and intelligent. We talk about great and greater, good and better, nice and nicer, fast and faster, dumb and dumber. Nothing, it seems, escapes the critical, compare-and-contrast mindset bred into our culture and constantly reinforced with our choice of language.

Do not make the mistake of thinking just because judgment is so commonplace it's harmless. If you do, you are likely to accept it as an innocent part of our lives without questioning the effect it has on our mental, emotional, and physical health. If you mistake its confining nature, you will stay caught in its grasp and might even view this sickness as useful and necessary. It is neither. It is illness: Judgmentalillness.

This illness narrows our vision and solidifies perspective. It traps us in our own judgmental language. We spend our present moments determining if people, places, or things meet our mental models of how they should be. When our judgments reveal their shortcomings, we create frustration, anxiety, disappointment, and stress for ourselves. In essence, when we judge, we sabotage our own happiness.

Consider what happens when we judge other people. Charlie began running at age sixty-five. He participated in his first 10K race nine months later. His initial one-hour adventure in competitive running turned out to be a full-blown excursion in comparison. As people passed him, Charlie judged. He judged others and he judged himself.

"She's got a big butt. How can she move that fast?"

"I must be a slowpoke if that guy can pass me."

"In terms of speed, I'm pathetic."

When a woman pushing a stroller passed him at the four-mile mark, he thought, "I am one dead ass when it comes to running."

Somewhere in the race, Charlie switched from judging competitors to judging the spectators.

> "I may be slow, but at least I'm not seventy pounds overweight like that guy sitting in the lawn chair with his gut hanging out."
>
> "What a bunch of couch potatoes."
>
> "That woman doesn't look like she can run to the corner and back. Talk about out of shape!"

Charlie's mind was so busy churning out evaluations that he effectively missed the whole race. He kept projecting his judgments outward and failed to look inward to see what he personally was feeling and experiencing.

Whether running a road race, working in an office, or driving down the road, judgment limits how we see people.

"That kid is lazy."

"My boss is disorganized."

"My coworker is a flirt."

When you judge another person as lazy and use self-talk or talk out loud in a way that reflects that view, you strengthen your belief that she is in fact lazy. What follows is a string of mental processes that serve to prove you're correct. Your repetitious judgments, now turned into a solid belief, work like an alarm ready to go off internally anytime you perceive "lazy." Because of your strengthened belief that this person is lazy, you're more likely to notice behaviors that could be interpreted as lazy. Ambitious acts are less likely to be noticed or, if noticed at all, are not categorized as ambitious.

Using selective noticing and biased interpretation, you create a distorted and narrow picture of this person in your mind. You prove to yourself that your judgment is correct. The person is lazy and you have your observations to prove it. *Abracadabra.*

Judgmentalillness is working full force, and not on your behalf. Your judgment prevents you from seeing clearly. You don't often notice this person's passion, fear, doubts, kindness, thoughtfulness, honesty, or other characteristics that make her the complex human being she is. You have turned her into a label rather than a young woman displaying a variety of attitudes and behaviors.

Judgment categorizes. It serves to draw a mental cage around the person from which they cannot escape in your view. If you judge your coworker as a flirt, you look at him through biased eyes. You don't notice or dwell on the times he methodically prepares a sales presentation, brings a professional attitude to the meeting, or treats the opposite sex with courtesy and respect. Because your language of judgment lumps him into the "flirt" category, your mind produces an all-inclusive picture of him as "that way."

Another characteristic of Judgmentalillness is that it tends to make permanent. Your judgments become self- fulfilling and cement the person in place, exactly where you placed them with your thoughts. If you judge your child as a troublemaker and use words that pass that belief on to him, you have just increased the likelihood that he will make trouble in the future. If you create your boss as unorganized in your mind, he will become unorganized in the reality you create for yourself. That belief flows from your thoughts and the perceptions of disorganization which follow. Once your boss has become disorganized in your mind, he must become extraorganized before you release him from the mental constraints you've placed on him.

Another way you create dis-ease for yourself using judgments is that you simply don't have enough information to make accurate assumptions. We judge on the basis of insufficient data. We don't really know what it's like to be in another person's skin. We haven't lived their life experiences or seen the world through their eyes.

We have one ride in a rental car and judge it as a piece of junk. We watch the wide receiver drop two passes and classify him as a bum. We have one trip to a vacation resort and judge it as excellent. We meet our child's teacher for a half-hour conference and come away with several judgments about him and how he handles his professional practice.

Are you judging your own parents? If so, you are doing it with incomplete data. Do you know what it was like to live through the Korean War and the march on Selma, Alabama? Do you know how your parents were parented? Are you certain about their hopes, dreams, fears, and goals? You didn't live their life experiences. They did and you didn't. You don't know everything.

Take something as simple as the weather. The weather doesn't decide to arrive in our life each day as bad or good. It just comes with no evaluation attached to it. Sometimes it comes as rain, sometimes as snow. It shows up as cloudy, sunny, ten degrees or ninety degrees. It just comes to us as it is, free of judgment and evaluation. We are the ones who, in the depths of our minds, judge the weather. We say:

"It's a lousy day today."

"We had crummy weather on our vacation."

"The weatherman said it was going to be a good day today."

"I love this string of great weather."

"When is this terrible weather ever going to end?"

When it rains and you use words that evaluate it negatively (lousy, awful, terrible, pitiful), your evaluation is more than just inaccurate. Your choice of language sets in motion forces that create a reality that matches your evaluation. When it rains and you call it lousy, you narrow that day in your mind. That process of restricting occurs because your belief system filters are now on alert quietly scanning for proof that your judgment is accurate. Your powerful mind goes right to work for you, sending you a steady flow of thoughts and perceptions that match your inaccurate and incomplete judgment. The end result is the creation of an illusion about the day. You have turned a rainy day into a lousy day and you are caught up in Judgmentalillness.

When you judge the day as lousy, your mind creates dis-ease by focusing on limitation. It will produce an endless stream of all the things you can't do because it's raining. Opportunities lost become your mantra and your focus. You see the rain as inconvenient. It's preventing you from completing goals. It's keeping you from doing what you wanted. Separating emotions of sadness, disgust, frustration, irritation, and disappointment are activated. Sure enough, it's a lousy day. Almost like magic.

When you don't judge the rain as good or bad, when you just talk about it as rain and don't evaluate it in any way, you widen the day for yourself. Now, because your mind is not searching to prove something to you, it can send you a larger selection of thoughts and perceptions about the day. At this point, you're more likely to think about new possibilities offering a wider range of choices. A walk in the rain, enjoying the sounds of rain on the roof, or cleaning out a closet might surface as ideas now. When this happens, there is a greater chance you will shut down stress and activate healthy emotions of joy, happiness, and peace. The previous dis-ease of Judgmentalillness has now been replaced by contentment and adventure.

Good day or bad day? That's about you. It's not about the day. The day just shows up. It isn't anything until you create it a certain way in your mind.

How you interpret the weather tells more about you that it does about the weather. How you judge your child's behavior gives others more information about you than about your child's behavior. How you see your coworker is about you, your thoughts, your belief system, and the reality you choose to create.

As you know, *The Abracadabra Effect: 13 Verbally Transmitted Diseases and How to Cure Them* is the title of this book. What you might not know is that we solicited feedback on this title from over 100 friends, relatives, and past customers.

Some said it was great, fantastic, or brilliant. One person said, "It's a stroke of genius." Another announced emphatically, "I'm buying no book that talks about diseases." Someone said they didn't understand the title. Other comments we received include:

"I'd like to think about it."

"What are the other choices?"

"I love it."

"When can I buy one?"

"Are you sure you have abracadabra spelled right?"

"Awesome."

"That will sell a million copies."

"I don't think it will sell."

"That's an attention-getter."

"I don't think it will attract enough attention."

"People won't understand it."

"I get it. Wow!"

We received a variety of reactions to our book title. Why is it there are so many different judgments when there is only one title? The answer is pretty simple. There are different reactions to our title because each person hearing it hears it through their own unique set of filters. Each person's mind contains different beliefs, thoughts, words, values, and experiences. And since we all filter what we hear and see through our minds, we each create a unique interpretation.

Judgments are not about the thing being judged. They are always about the person doing the judging. Each person who judged our title gave us some information about the title. They gave us more information about themselves: what they value, what they care about, what they see as important.

The primary message you send to others when you judge is: "I am a person who likes to judge." That's about you.

Do you recall the last time you were around a person exhibiting high levels of Judgmentalillness? Chances are they were judging someone who was not present. So who do you think they talked about after you left? Fear and suspicion that others are judging you is another form of dis-ease that results from Judgmentalillness. Because you judge, you tend to think others judge, too.

In this case, your words behave like a boomerang. If you send out judgment, you attract judgment in return. If you send out kindness, you attract more of that. By reducing your evaluations and stepping out of the judgment trap for extended periods of time, you will end worry about how others are judging you.

Your judgments about other people rarely change them. Instead, they change you. They change you from a pain-free person to one who has now inflicted himself with dis-ease. Even if you keep your judgments to yourself, those judgments affect your energy and impact your relationships in a negative way. The quantity and the quality of your interactions with the person you're judging are altered accordingly.

Are you tired of the ill effects of your addiction to judging? Do you want to reduce the inflammation caused by Judgmentalillness in your life? Are you ready to step out of the judgment trap and into healthy living? Consider the prescriptions below.

Prescription 1

Stay around healthy people. If you have been a judger, you can be sure you have attracted other judgers into your life. Judgers attract judgers. They will show up in your office before the morning meeting and invite you to join them in the evaluation game. Since you have been a judge in the past, they will expect you to join in.

Get out of there. Go use the restroom, get a cup of coffee, or close your door, telling your coworker you have a task to complete before the meeting. If you cannot escape physically, escape in your mind. Think about something else while they go on about how unfair your supervisor is. Challenge yourself to say nothing. Keep your lips sealed. Don't even give them a head nod. Even nonverbal reactions encourage others to continue with their judgments.

Notice their judging without evaluating it. Notice what it sounds like. Remind yourself that this is the style of language you are committed to eliminating in your life. Refuse to judge it.

Prescription 2

Learn to describe. Replace judgment with description.

"The weather is crappy" judges. "It's ten degrees with a wind chill of minus thirteen" describes.

"She's lazy" judges. "She waited until the last minute to begin her homework" describes.

"This car is a piece of junk" judges. "There is little tread on the tires and the air conditioner doesn't work" describes.

Describing the behavior of another person does not brand them as "that way." It simply states what their behavior was one time.

"He's a liar" announces to yourself and others that that is who he is. It gives the impression that lying is part of his being. "He didn't tell the truth on his expense form" describes a behavior he chose last week. It is not who he is. It is what he did once.

"She's thoughtless" is your judgment branding your neighbor as uncaring. "She didn't send a sympathy card to Eduardo when his mother passed" describes a behavior. Notice that the description is free of evaluation. It simply describes the action or, in this case, lack of action. It does not rate it or judge it.

When you spill food on yourself at dinner, refuse to announce, "I'm such a slob." Describe instead. Say, "Oh, I spilled some salad dressing on my shirt. Oh well, that happens sometimes." Yes, it happens sometimes. It is not who you are or what you do every time. Choose words that describe.

Prescription 3

Practice, practice, practice. Overdose on practice.

Are you judging this prescription? Practice.

Do you think your children are being disrespectful? Practice.

Are you still thinking about abracadabra? Practice.

Are you judging yourself for not practicing? Practice.

Practice will not make perfect. It will make permanent.

Practice.

Chapter 12
The Rightabolic Syndrome

One payoff people often get from prolonged Judgmentalillness is acute activation of the "Rightabolic Syndrome." People judge because that behavior produces an important and valuable benefit. It has a major payoff. They get to be right.

The Rightabolic Syndrome defined: The state of having to be right, which breeds comparison, evaluation, and alienation. Characterized by the generation of ill feelings, the digging in of heels, and mental and physical distancing.

Being right is a reward we get from judging. If you judge your coworker as a spy and later notice her communicating information concerning another employee to your supervisor, you prove you are right. When you label the marketing retreat incredible and get others to support that interpretation, you are right. When you blame your spouse for her poor budgeting and the family runs out of money between paychecks . . . (you know where we're going with this). Again, you get to be right.

Confirmation of rightness feels good. That's why the Rightabolic Syndrome is often misdiagnosed and not always seen as producing dis-ease. What could possibly be unhealthy about proving your worth to yourself?

Think of it this way. Eating half the chocolate cake feels good for the moment. So does eating fifteen ribs cooked with your mother's famous recipe. Buying that new truck on an impulse felt pretty good, too, didn't it? Just like that last shot of Tequila, the shot of self-worth you get from being right may feel good for the moment. The price you pay, though, may be greater that you realize.

First, being right doesn't work. Go ahead and judge your seminar leader as boring. Concentrate on all the things she does that prove your judgment to yourself. At the end of the day you get to walk out of the seminar being right. Congratulations. You just managed to create a boring day for yourself. Did being right help you learn any new management techniques? No. Did it facilitate the learning of ways to improve customer service? No. Are you more informed now than you were at the beginning of the day? Not likely. Do you get to be right? Yes. Congratulations. *Abracadabra.*

Maybe you don't like the house your spouse prefers to buy and you judge it as a time-consuming fix-up project. And you purchase it anyway, knowing you are right. Because you are unconsciously suffering from the Rightabolic Syndrome, you aren't aware you prove to yourself every day that this house is a fix-up project of huge proportions. You notice the old wallpaper, the paint peeling off the wall, and cupboards that don't completely close. You perceive the door to the deck as being in the wrong location. The wood floors seem to be calling to be refinished. The windows are out of date and energy inefficient. You sure are right about that old house. So what?

Does being right help you enjoy your home in this present moment? Is being right improving your relationship with your spouse? Does it help you generate feelings of joy, happiness, peace, and harmony? Does it help you relax? Or does it allow you to create dis-ease as your thoughts continue to churn out proof of your rightness?

The Rightabolic Syndrome alienates us from others. Setting up our inner world so we get to be right in our outer world fosters differences rather than commonalities. This "me versus them" attitude creates mental separation. Feelings of togetherness and cooperation suffer as we distance ourselves from other people with our steady march toward being right.

It's difficult to be right and cooperate simultaneously. It takes "me and them" thinking to create cooperation and the resulting togetherness. With a "me versus them" mindset, we create conflict and stress for ourselves. Comparing, evaluating, judging, and proving ourselves right invites the dis-ease of anxiety and turmoil to enter our lives. If we chase around all day proving our judgments to ourselves, fatigue and exhaustion are often the result.

If you hear yourself making any of the following comments, you could be stricken with the Rightabolic Syndrome.

"That's impossible."

"You're wrong about that."

"No way!"

"You're mistaken."

"You can't be right."

"There is not a chance that you could be correct about that."

"I've lived a lot longer than you have and I'm right about this. You'll see."

Do you desire to take the Rightabolic Syndrome to new heights? Do you want to inflame the need to be right to the point of extreme discomfort? Add this phrase to your language patterns: "I told you so."

If having unhealthy relationships, both at work and at home, is what you desire, "I told you so" will get you there fast. It's divisive and builds resentment. It invites irritation, annoyance, and emotional attacks.

"If you don't stop at this gas station, you'll run out of gas," Pablo was informed by his wife Bonita. Pablo looked at the gas gauge and decided to keep driving. When the car began to sputter twenty minutes later, Pablo eased it gently off the road. "I told you so" were the first words out of his wife's mouth.

When Pablo felt the car chugging, he knew what was happening. He didn't need anyone pointing out to him who was right and who was wrong in that moment. That was obvious. Bonita's "I told you so" aggravated the situation. In addition, it focused Pablo's attention outward to the person he felt was rubbing it in rather than facing toward problem solving and finding the best possible solution.

As Pablo stood by the road attempting to hitch a ride to the closest gas station, his resentment grew. So did his anger, bitterness, and hurt feelings.

Are you someone who frequently says, "I told you so"? If you are, consider that you are spreading dis-ease to others. Is what you get from reminding the other person you were right worth the price you pay in returned resentment and damage to the relationship? Is your need to be right stronger than your desire to spread the health generated by empathy and encouragement?

Bite your tongue when you find yourself in situations where you're tempted to say, "I told you so." Smile inwardly to yourself if your need to be right is surfacing. Have a silent moment of satisfaction if you must, and then let it go. Say nothing. Now is the time to send love and caring to your partner or coworker. Remember, being right doesn't work.

Prescription

When you notice the desire to be right protruding into your consciousness, nip it in the bud with one of the following sentences. You don't have to believe them. Just say them. Do this often enough and you'll believe them in time.

"You could be right about that."

"I don't think so and you might be correct."

"Your answer is one possibility."

"I definitely disagree and your answer could be the correct one."

"You might be right. I don't think so and you might be."

Use these health-producing responses when you absolutely know you are correct. You know the advertising department will reject the idea, and your coworker thinks they'll love it. You know your child will be watching from the sidelines at his taekwondo class because of the ketchup on his uniform, and he thinks no one will notice. You know the '85 Bears won the Super Bowl, and your neighbor disagrees.

"You could be right, and I remember Master Gary dismissing one student last week because of a dirty uniform" allows for the possibility that your child could be right. It does not make him wrong while you make yourself right. It demonstrates respect for his opinion while stating your own. It might well prevent you from eating crow later should his idea prove to be correct.

"I suppose they could like the idea, and I remember them being opposed to animation during the last advertising campaign" comes across as less rigid than "You're wrong about that." It reveals you as an employee who can keep an open mind and consider other possibilities even when you think you are correct.

Perhaps you think you and your spouse, coworker, or child like to argue and have fun proving each other wrong. Maybe it feels energizing to you. Perhaps you believe it creates no dis-ease in your relationships. You could be right about that, and we don't think so.

Chapter 13
Blameopoly

"He's got no one to blame but himself."

"The referees screwed us over."

"It's the mailroom people's fault."

"It's his father's fault. He's too permissive when our son is with him."

"The boss blew this one. He wasn't prepared for the presentation."

"The mechanic should have fixed this. That's what I paid for."

When you hear yourself or someone else finding fault or assigning blame, you can rest assured Blameopoly is flourishing.

Blameopoly defined: A language technique used to assign responsibility to someone or something else for the conditions that exist in one's life. An often unnoticed mind trick that allows one to think and behave unself-responsibly.

When you blame, you give away your personal power. Blaming conditions your mind to focus on others. Blaming effectively prevents you from examining any role you played in a given situation. It keeps responsibility on the backs of others and frees you to judge and activate separating emotions of anger, annoyance, and disgust. If you blame your boss, coworkers, spouse, children, parents, the government, your doctor, or anyone else for your problems, you give them your power. You leave them in control and render yourself impotent. Not a useful condition to have.

If you got a call from school informing you that your child fell and broke a leg, you would go to school as quickly as you could. Upon entering the school you would immediately start asking questions to find out whose fault it was. You would collect several versions of the situation and assign blame to those you deem responsible.

No, you wouldn't. Not unless the Blameopoly dis-ease had you so weak and delirious that your brain and heart were barely functioning. You would go immediately to the hospital emergency room and rush to the bedside of your daughter. You would nurture and reassure, helping your daughter feel as safe and loved as possible. Any time you invested in Blameopoly would distract from your efforts to be attentive to your child. Any time or energy you devoted to blaming and fault finding would waste valuable seconds you could use talking to the doctor, making decisions about possible surgery, and considering other options.

In an emergency, blame and fault finding serve no useful function. Nor are they helpful in our daily lives.

In what ways does blaming your boss for blowing the presentation help fix the situation? How does it help him improve the presentation next time? It doesn't. Finding fault with the employees in the mailroom does little to encourage you to look at the role you played in causing the package to be late. Blaming the mechanic for not fixing the car correctly does nothing to solve the problem with the steering wheel. Actually, it delays you from working together to design a plan to prevent it from occurring in the future.

Perhaps you're like Shingo, who got pulled over one night for driving across the yellow line. The police officer asked him to step out of his car, and when he did, a small bag fell to the ground. That small bag contained an ounce of marijuana.

Shingo explained vociferously to the officer the bag was not his. His story was that he'd given his friend a ride home from school earlier that day. "It must have been his," Shingo exclaimed. At the police station, Shingo was asked to provide a urine sample. That test detected traces of marijuana in his system. Also in his system, though not revealed by the test, were huge doses of Blameopoly. Shingo continued his denial by saying that some of his friends smoke weed and it must have gotten into his system through second-hand smoke.

Later, Shingo was placed on probation and given a meeting time to discuss his probation with the officer in charge of his case. He didn't appear at the meeting. His explanation? "No one told me the correct time for the meeting." On another occasion, Shingo failed to show up for his first court date. He blamed it on a friend who was supposed to give him a ride and didn't show up to get him.

Shingo is clearly suffering from an acute case of Blameopoly. Is there hope for him? Of course. And it will be important for him to begin accepting responsibility for his actions rather than blaming others.

While we hope Shingo learns to accept responsibility and stop assigning fault to others, we also want him to learn that blaming himself is not healthy either.

"It was my fault."

"There is nobody to blame but me."

"I'm willing to accept the blame. I'm the one at fault here."

Stop it. Blaming yourself isn't any more effective than blaming someone else. If you want to take responsibility, we accept that. Taking responsibility means noticing the role you played in creating a situation, learning from it, and moving on by taking corrective action. It does not involve beating yourself up, being critical, or engaging in self-rejection. If you are indeed responsible, stand up and own it without adding blame or fault to the mix.

Are you mentally pointing fingers at someone in your life right now? Do you hear yourself using or thinking words that blame yourself or others? If so, it might be time to treat that dis-ease and move one big step forward in your action to end Blameopoly. It might be time to fill and use the following prescription.

Prescription

To end Blameopoly, learn about and use the "Own It" injection regularly. It will help you take responsibility for what is happening in your life.

Own It is a technique to use when you feel like a victim—when you notice that you are feeling unfairly treated and sense you are about to assign blame. Instead of focusing on what the other person did to you or how they created the situation you find yourself in, give yourself an Own It injection by examining all the decisions you had control over, things you did to set it up, ways you contributed to the final result, and choices you had along the way. Assigning blame and finding fault are not the focus here. Response-ability is the issue. Where were you responsible in this present scenario? Where could you have altered the course? Where could you have made a difference? What could you have done?

A friend of ours, we'll call him Bill because that's not his name and he knows us, had a travel agent who once messed up on a free ticket he had intended to use to fly cross country. It appeared as though the agent's error would cost him hundreds of dollars and/or end his plans to attend a week-long retreat. Bill was livid, blaming her in his mind for being uninformed, not following through, and not being professional. He was creating dis-ease, manifesting stress while immobilizing himself by activating blame and judgment, all directed squarely at her. After all, it was her fault.

In the midst of annoyance, anger, and self-inflicted pain, Bill remembered the Own It injection. He began to look at where and how he had helped create the predicament he was now in. He realized he had picked the agent from a variety of travel agents available. He was clearly responsible for that decision. Bill also realized he had not chosen to read the back of the free ticket coupon. He neglected to look for blackout dates. He had also chosen to wait until one week before his travel date to check with his travel agent and make sure everything was under control.

By giving himself an Own It injection, Bill began to own (take responsibility for) the situation. No blame, no fault, and no guilt. Just responsibility. As soon as Bill took responsibility for the role he had played in creating the situation, he began to calm down. He stopped stressing himself. Consequently, he was better able to enter a space conducive to solution seeking. Bill called the agent back and they were able to construct an alternate plan that did cost some dollars and allowed him to go through with his travel plans.

What are you stewing about right now? Who are you blaming? Are you mad at the auto mechanic? Do you have a relative who you think is at fault? Own It and see if you don't change your mind about the situation.

Over time, using the Own It prescription will reduce stress, enhance solution seeking, and increase your sense of personal power. If it doesn't, don't blame us. Own it.

Chapter 14
Needatonin

"I need a vacation."

"I need a new job."

"I need to go on a diet."

"I need some respect from my coworkers."

"I need _____ (fill in the blank)."

Do you want to feel more personal power in your life and reduce the dis-ease of Needatonin? If so, push the delete button on the word "need" in your vocabulary list and reverse the effect that Needatonin produces in your life.

Needatonin definited: A whiny verbal skill that increases dependency. A way of announcing that you want to be taken care of. An effort to manipulate others.

Food, water, and love. Those are the only three needs that exist in our world. Everything else is not a need. It is a want or desire.

You do not *need* a new job. You may dislike the one you have. You may be unfulfilled and performing menial tasks far below your capability. Your boss may verbally abuse you. Still, your life won't end if you do not get a new job. It is not a need. It's a want. A strong want perhaps—and it is still a want.

You don't really *need* respect from your coworkers. Clearly you deserve respect. And you will survive if you don't get it. You might not be thrilled about it, and you can exist without it.

"You don't understand," you may argue. "I really, really want a new job." Oh, you *want* a new job? That's different. Yes, when you push the delete button on "need," replace it with the word "want."

You don't really *need* a vacation. You *want* a vacation.

You don't *need* more respect from your coworkers. You *want* more respect.

You don't *need* a bigger office. You *want* a bigger office.

You don't *need* a raise. And you probably *want* a raise starting today. OK. We're with you on that.

What's the big fuss about changing "need" to "want"? Consider there are two main ways to describe the desires of your life: "I need" and "I want." "Need" and "want" are the articulated words, whether you speak them aloud or silently to yourself. Pay attention to the unspoken, silent message you communicate when you use one or the other. One promotes dis-ease, the other spreads health.

"I need" sends out vibrations of dependency. It often has a whiny ring to it. As you increase your need for someone or something, you also increase the strength of your dependency. As your dependency grows, your sense of personal power withers.

If you need your coworkers to be more respectful so you can feel good about yourself, you transfer the responsibility for your self-esteem from you to them. If you need a new job to find meaning and create passion in your work life, you have given away your responsibility for creating it where you are presently employed. In each case, you limit your response-ability.

There are expectations (one of the silent messages) that accompany uttering, "I need." When you proclaim "I need" something, it's as if you expect someone else to come along and fill that need for you. And since you expect someone to fix it for you, you are less likely to make an active move to see that it happens and more likely to assume a passive stance.

On the other hand, "I want" communicates independence. It's a more self-sufficient expression and has no expectation attached to it. Since there is no expectation, a more active stance is usually forthcoming, making it more likely you will take steps to move toward fulfillment of that desire.

Think about this: do you want your employees *wanting* you as their boss or *needing* you as their boss? Do you prefer to be in a state of *needing* respect or *wanting* respect from your coworkers? Do you want your spouse to *want* you or *need* you? Be aware that there are no right or wrong answers to these questions. Also, stay conscious that "need" has more dependency dis-ease attached to it than "want" does. "Want" carries more independence. If you want dependent employees, a dependent spouse, or dependent children, you can have that. You get to choose. *Abracadabra.*

Do you desire employees (spouse, children, coworkers) who *want* or *need* approval? If they *need* approval, they will be more anxious to please. They will tell you what they think you want to hear on a regular basis. They will tiptoe around, afraid to say things you might disagree with. If your employees *need* approval, they will agree with you when they really disagree. They will negate their own self-interests and beliefs and go along with yours. You gain compliance and you lose an effective alternative voice in your organization.

If your employees *want* rather than *need* approval, they will behave differently. They will ask for it if that is what they desire. They won't measure their self-worth by whether you agree with them or not. They won't take disagreement personally. They won't be immobilized if they don't get approval. After all, they don't *need* approval. They *want* it.

"I *need* you."

"I *need* it tonight."

"I *need* you to do something for me."

"I *need* you to listen to me."

Have you heard any of these lines? They're not examples of clear, open, honest communication. The word "need" is being used to manipulate. And the target of the manipulation is *you.* These statements want you to feel responsible for fulfilling someone else's desires. They're an attempt to dispense guilt.

Imagine being single and having a person of the opposite sex come up to you at a party, pull you aside privately, and say, "I need you." We're not sure what you would do. We do know what we would do. RUN!

Neither of us wants to be in a dependent relationship. We don't intend to join up with someone who announces their neediness. We're not willing to allow ourselves to be in a position of being responsible for someone else's desires, sexual or otherwise. The dis-ease and ill health that accompanies a dependent, manipulative relationship has no appeal for us.

However, if we were not currently in satisfying, affirming, uplifting relationships and that same person came up and announced, "I want you," we might consider joining in the conversation.

"I *want* a new car."

"I *want* a raise."

"I *want* a soul mate."

"I *want* to be free of verbally transmitted dis-eases."

Does that sound selfish to you? Consider the following question: "Who wants to go around saying, 'I want this' and 'I want that' all the time? You sound like a spoiled brat." That's a reaction we received from a workshop participant recently. Here is our answer.

We see a major difference between selfishness and self-fullness. Selfishness occurs when you make choices and don't care what happens to anyone else. We do not recommend or encourage that stance. We firmly believe in self-fullness. If you are feeling full and experiencing overflow, you have more to give to your family, your colleagues, your work, and the universe. If you are not feeling full, you are operating from perceived lack. Therefore, you feel you have less to give.

If you are low on self-esteem, positive energy, and personal power, you will be less inclined to give to others. You will use what you have for your own benefit. Your behaviors will flow from a "not enough" belief system, and that dis-ease could result in hoarding what you do have.

On the other hand, you could take care of yourself by satisfying some of your own wants. You could buy that new shirt and tie. Looking good and feeling good on the inside gives you more excitement to share during the day and during your afternoon presentation. When you return from that weekend getaway to a cabin in the woods, you come back relaxed and refreshed and now have more energy to distribute to the universe.

When you pay to have your car detailed and smelling like new again, a bounce in your step accompanies you on your next sales call. Since how you treat others often reflects how you feel about yourself, it could well be a disservice to others to deny caring for yourself by satisfying some of your own wants.

Balance is important here. Yes, it's useful to invest some time and money on taking care of yourself. You deserve it. And when you are self-full, those minutes and dollars spent will touch the other important people in your life.

It is critical, though, to fit your wants into the context of interdependence. Every dollar you invest in you is one less dollar you have available to spend on your spouse or children. Every hour you use relaxing in the hot tub is one hour not available to work on the new advertising campaign. Satisfy some of your wants. And temper them with the realization that you are connected to your family and coworkers.

Prescription 1

Once again, the dis-ease of anxiety, stress, and decreased response-ability is located in the mind. And words make minds. So re-mind yourself by changing "need" to "want."

When you hear yourself saying, "I *need* you to meet with him this afternoon," stop. Immediately change your words to "I *want* you to meet with him this afternoon."

Change "I *need* to convince her" to "I *want* to convince her."

Change "I *need* a new computer" to "I *want* a new computer."

"That's too simple," you might be thinking. Change your mind about that, too. Remember, nothing is *too* anything. Yes, it is simple. Change your words to change your mind. Change your mind to change your world. Simple? Yes. And effective? Also yes. *Abracadabra.*

You are in charge of your mind. You are its primary programmer. Take charge of the words you put in there. Manage your own mind to manage your reality and your world.

Prescription 2

Speak up for yourself. Express your wants. Only a few of us live or work with psychics. Chances are you aren't one of them. We don't hang out with psychics, yet we often act like we do. We clutch our wants tightly, don't express them, and then upset ourselves because other people don't figure them out and do something about them. We run around expecting people to read our minds by peering through our nonexistent glass heads.

You know you're activating the myth of the glass head when you think thoughts like, "My boss should know I need attention" and "If she really cared, she'd figure it out." Then when our boss doesn't figure it out or give us attention, we resent it. "If he loved me he'd know" and "If you don't know I'm not going to tell you" are other signs that you are engaging the myth of the glass head.

One sure way to drastically reduce getting what you want is to fail to verbalize it. If you're the only one that knows you want a back rub, a new coffee maker, or an opportunity to address the staff at the next meeting, your odds of getting it aren't high.

Reduce the risk of not creating what you want. Speak up for yourself. Put your response-ability out there where everyone can see and hear you using it.

Prescription 3

When implementing prescriptions 1 and 2, attitude and tone are critical. "I wants" are not to be delivered in a whiny tone. Use your mature adult voice when stating them. The goal is to give honest and direct information so others will know what you are thinking and feeling. Maintain an attitude that does not convey you have to have your want fulfilled or even expect it. This prescription is a way of giving others information about you so you can begin a useful dialogue with them.

Your "I want" is best delivered as a preference rather than as a demand. Saying "I want" is another way of communicating, "I would like it if," or "I'd prefer it if." The message you are really sending is, "This is what I want. Tell me what you want. Let's talk it over and see if we can reach consensus."

We want you to change your needs to wants and observe what happens to them over time.

We want you to enjoy the process of satisfying your wants while simultaneously diminishing the suffering of craving and frustration.

We want you to become need-less and want-full.

We want you to experience joy instead of the self-inflicted dis-ease of Needatonin.

That's what we want. What do you want?

Chapter 15
Fungatious Feedback

"Good job on that presentation, Charlie."

"This is an excellent report."

"I made a stupid shot on the third fairway."

"You were rude to your grandfather yesterday, Mario."

"The car looked beautiful after you washed it."

"That's a fantastic idea."

"Your position paper went flat at the end."

"I thought the PowerPoint presentation was weak."

The statements above were made by different people in vastly different situations. Despite their differences, the examples all have one thing in common. Each is feedback that is ripe with unhealthy fungus.

Fungatious Feedback definition: Providing information that is primarily evaluative. Filled with judgment. Lacking specifics and void of constructive information. Failure to feed forward.

The number one behavior modification tool used in businesses, schools, and homes today is praise. Parents use it. Educators use it. Managers use it.

Praise itself has been praised in books, seminars, and webinars by educators, parenting experts, and management consultants. The use of praise has become so universal it's difficult to find anyone who is against it.

Praise is good. Everyone knows that. Employees tell us they would like to hear more praise. Parents tell us their children are motivated by praise. Educators say they use praise to build self-esteem and confidence in their students.

Praise is good. We just said that. So let's say it one more time. Praise is good. Is it really? Or is that simply an assumption?

Praise is good.

Praise builds self-esteem.

Praise is motivational.

Assumptions one and all. Assumptions that are not often questioned. Assumptions that most of us accept without thinking about them. Assumptions that often go unchallenged.

No more! The assumption challengers have arrived. And we are here to ask you, "What if . . . ?"

What if praise is not so good? Aspirin is good. Is more aspirin better? Can't aspirin be administered haphazardly, even dangerously? Yes, it can. And we intend to make the point that praise can be administered haphazardly, even dangerously, also.

What if praise does not build self-esteem? What if it just helps the receiver feel good for the moment and disappears quickly? What if it builds dependence, requiring the receiver to chase it so they can obtain another fix? Sounds like a drug to us.

What if praise is not motivational? What if the praise we send works to prevent the receiver from developing internal motivation and teaches them to rely on external forces for motivation? That sounds like Fungatious Feedback to us.

Would you like to become a healing force in the universe? If so, it's time to take a closer look at praise and adopt ways to administer it in healthy and helpful doses.

There are three types of praise. Two of them help people build a strong internal sense of self-esteem and self-motivation. Two out of three are free of the infectious fungus that feeds dependence and delays growth in self-responsibility. One out of the three is, in our opinion, harmful. It is also the one most frequently used.

The three types of praise are *evaluative*, *descriptive*, and *appreciative*. The root word of each tells its function.

Evaluative praise evaluates.

Descriptive praise describes.

Appreciative praise appreciates.

If you praise with evaluative praise, your language is full of words like "good," "excellent," "fantastic," "beautiful," "wonderful," "incredible," "outstanding," "super," and "tremendous." When you use praise that evaluates, whether talking to yourself or to others, your words are a judgmental interpretation of the recipient's product, idea, suggestion, character, appearance, behavior, or accomplishment.

People who are starving for recognition will happily accept evaluative praise. It helps them feel good for the moment. A few doses of evaluative praise and they're hooked. When the "feel good" wears off, they begin to chase it. They go in search of another fix. Their dis-ease, which manifests as uneasiness, anxiety, and nervousness, itches until a scratcher arrives to administer a quick-to-fade remedy of more evaluative praise.

One danger of evaluative praise is that heavy exposure to it results in the victim learning to see others as the major source of approval in his or her life. In addition, the small shots of self-esteem they receive are being administered from the outside in. This results in a self-esteem dependence on the evaluations of others. Without constant reminders delivered in the harmless-appearing wrappings of evaluative praise, these people are not sure of their own worth.

One other flaw associated with evaluative praise is that it fails to teach anything that can be used in the future. So your boss told you the company newsletter you edit was "awesome" last week. What was awesome about it? And why was it interpreted as awesome? Knowing that information would give you some data you could put to use later. Did the newsletter focus on two important company objectives? Which ones? Was it humorous, informative, or grammatically correct? Hearing it was "awesome" only tells you one thing: that one person rated it so. You have no idea why.

Did you tell your spouse she's a good listener? If you did, you gave her little information and one huge evaluation. Plus, you have positioned yourself above her as her judge. Nobody likes being judged. It is a big me/little you position that invites resentment and resistance.

Tell your spouse, "I like the way you listen to me and hear me out without interrupting. I like knowing I can express my anger without you taking it personally. I appreciate the time you give to hearing my concerns. Thank you." If you use this style of language, you have begun applying one of the most effective "medications" for curing Fungatious Feedback. You have crossed the judgmental line of evaluative praise and moved into the territory of descriptive and appreciative praise.

Prescription 1

Descriptive praise describes. Use it liberally with friends, family, coworkers, and yourself. This style of praise speaks to accomplishments. It describes rather than evaluates what was seen or heard.

"You had over 100 orders to get out this morning and you did it all before 11 o'clock."

"You got right to the main point in your report, and the facts you added strengthened your position."

"You came and told me directly, and you did it with personal ownership and without finger pointing."

Notice the absence of evaluation in the descriptive praise examples above. You won't find any "good jobs" or "excellent work" hidden in there. When you choose words that describe the situation, you allow the person hearing the words to draw their own conclusion. You leave room for the evaluation to come from within. You don't attempt to fill them up with self-esteem. You allow them to create it from the inside out.

Prescription 2

Appreciative praise appreciates. This style of praise usually begins or ends with the words, "I appreciate," or "Thank you."

"Thank you for making the follow-up contacts with Mr. Wilson. He just ordered 300 dollars worth of new parts from us."

"Thank you, guys, for raking the leaves while I was gone. You saved me over an hour in my day. I appreciate it."

"Thank you for taking the time to share with us the specific problems you were having with the new machine. Your detailed explanation helped us find a solution that will prevent these problems from occurring in the future. I'm grateful."

Once again, you will not find any evaluative comments in these examples of appreciative praise. No judging of efforts, motivation, or results.

The appreciative praise prescription includes two parts. First, tell the person you appreciate their efforts. Second, tell the positive effect their behavior had on you, your family, or your organization.

"*Thank you, guys, for raking the leaves while I was gone.* (Appreciates the effort.) *You saved me over an hour in my day.* (Tells the effect it had on your life.) *I appreciate it.*"

"Thank you for taking the time to share with us the specific problems you were having with the new machine. (Appreciates.) *Your detailed explanation helped us find a solution that will prevent these problems from occurring in the future.* (Tells the effect it will have on your organization and future customer service issues.) *I'm grateful.*"

"Thank you for taking the leadership position on this project. (Appreciation.) *You freed me up to give the marketing department my full attention.* (The effect it had on you and the marketing department.)

When sharing what you appreciate, take care to comment only on specific acts. Steer clear of naming character traits, such as "trustworthy," "dependable," and "honest." Saying, "I appreciate your trustworthiness," is simply another way to evaluate a person. A comment like, "I appreciate you following through exactly as you said you would," allows the other person to say to himself, "I am trustworthy." The goal is to allow the recipient of the praise to do the rating on the inside. Use words that create room for him to draw the conclusion.

Prescription 3

Are you receiving repeated exposure to evaluative praise? Are you suffering the bloated feeling that results from people trying to fill you up with evaluations? Are you tired of their working to neutralize your internal evaluator and send it into a state of hibernation?

Ask people what they mean when they send evaluations your way. When your child says, "Dad, that was a great dinner you fixed," ask, "What do you mean by 'great'?" If a coworker tells you that you did an excellent job on the project, ask for clarification. "What did you think was excellent about it?" or "I'd like to hear specifically what you liked and why."

Find out what people mean by "tremendous," "beautiful," or "fantastic." Do not allow evaluative praise to be the only communication that feeds you. Ask for nourishing comments that deliver real information you can use.

Suppose the efforts or the results someone generates are not something you want to praise? Is there a way to give negative feedback that doesn't contribute to Fungatious Feedback?

Yes. Read on.

Chapter 16
Corrective Fungatious Feedback

At first glance, praise and criticism appear to be opposites. A closer examination will reveal they are simply two sides of the same coin. Do you want to give someone your two cents' worth? You can deliver it with praise or with criticism.

Criticism, like praise, can be delivered in evaluative, descriptive, or unappreciative terms.

"The meeting was terrible."

"The food was ordinary."

"The joke the speaker told was disgusting."

"Your homework and your notebook are sloppy."

The examples above are intended to give the receiver important feedback. The evaluative words "terrible," "ordinary," "disgusting," and "sloppy" are similar to their praise counterparts of "fantastic," "wonderful," "excellent," and "incredible" in that they all provide very little useful information.

What benefit is there to hearing that the meeting was terrible unless you know specifically what was terrible about it? What are you going to do with the information that the food was ordinary without knowing the exact details of what the person passing on this information is talking about? And just what did the person who told you about the joke choose to be disgusted by?

Criticism does little to move a person forward. If you want your feedback to promote maximal opportunity for change in the person receiving it, we suggest you perform a "word transplant." Remove criticism from your language patterns and replace it with corrective feedback. Criticism creates distance. Corrective feedback invites people to move forward.

Corrective feedback is necessary and important. When an employee's performance is below expectation, when your child fails to follow through with a commitment, when the washing machine you had repaired is still malfunctioning, it is time to give corrective feedback. If we don't give it, we communicate to others that any effort or result will do.

The message we are sending by not giving corrective feedback is:

"I didn't notice."

"I don't care."

"It doesn't matter."

It is not helpful to send those messages. Sending healthy, corrective feedback will be necessary from time to time. When you determine that it would be helpful to your organization, family, or personal life to send verbal messages of correction, consider the following:

Helpful correction that is free of dis-ease-spreading agents is specific.

Informing someone they did a poor job is evaluative and global. The information lacks specifics that would help the other person learn what it was that was poor about the job. Telling the washer repairperson the noise is still present when the machine moves to the rinse cycle gives her information she can use to improve her performance and the performance of the washer. Without specific knowledge, others are handicapped when attempting to correct mistakes and learn from them.

Dis-ease-free correction does not attack character or personality.

People often perceive evaluative feedback as an attack. They believe it is aimed directly at them and take it personally. Dis-ease symptoms of resentment, resistance, and defensiveness often follow. If you tailor your words to speak to the situation rather than the person, there is less chance he or she will choose to take offense. Choose words that focus on what was or was not accomplished, what is included or missing from your expectations, and what you specifically found helpful or unhelpful.

"Time sheets need to be filled out and turned in by Friday" focuses on a specific behavior. It describes what needs to be done. "You're forgetful" draws attention to the person and does not offer instruction. "This report does not have a recommendation in it" points to the situation. "You forgot to include a recommendation" puts the spotlight on the person.

"What's wrong with *you*?"

"*You're* not very organized, are *you*?"

"What were *you* thinking?"

"I don't believe *you* forgot that."

Healthy corrective feedback describes what needs to be improved.

"Putting a couple of customer testimonials right here would strengthen your point."

"When you go on vacation, it will be helpful if Wilson knows exactly what you have committed to our customers during that time period."

"It took a lot of time to read your book report, Connie. I had trouble reading the words. I couldn't make out some of them. Clear handwriting would make my role of checker a lot easier."

Think of corrective feedback as corrective feed forward. Design your communication so it feeds the person forward toward correction and improvement.

The main function of healthy corrective feedback is to make the expected outcome clear.

"Resource materials need to be returned to the shelf so others can use them when they want them."

"It's helpful for the next shift to have the tools cleaned and dried."

"Congratulating the other team after their victory is a ritual that celebrates the thrill of competition for both teams."

Notice that describing the expected outcome is different from telling the person what to do. "Clean the tools and get them ready for the next shift" tells them what to do. "It's helpful for the next shift to have the tools cleaned and dried" does not. This style of feedback contains the silent message, "I think you're smart enough to figure out a helpful response here."

Another way to give people healthy corrective feedback is to share your lack of appreciation.

"I didn't like cleaning up the sink before I began dinner."

"I don't appreciate having to hold up the newsletter because one article is missing."

"It's not fun for me to jump in the truck and realize it's low on gas."

People generally respond better when you share what you don't appreciate or describe what you don't like than they do if you criticize with evaluation. You'll get a better response with, "I don't appreciate pop cans and empty lunch sacks left in the lunchroom," than you will by saying, "The lunchroom is a mess." You'll attract more cooperation when your remark is, "I don't enjoy getting out this mailing alone," than when you say, "You're all lazy and inconsiderate."

Prescription 1

You can deactivate the spread of Fungatious Feedback with one simple prescription. The antidote is to use the number one rule of corrective feedback. That rule is: **Speak to the situation, not to the person.** Use a potent array of language that focuses on what was accomplished or not accomplished, what exists or doesn't exist, what you feel or don't feel. Leave the person out of it.

"Safety goggles belong on at all times."

"The plan to improve your grade in history is missing a paragraph on why the plan is important."

"There are empty juice cans and leftover pizza in the family room."

"Snow needs to be cleared from our sidewalk before we open for business."

Prescription 2

Use Prescription 1 morning, noon, and night—and everywhere in between. To prevent getting infected by the epidemic of Fungatious Feedback, use corrective feedback with your family, friends, coworkers, and anybody else you encounter. Not only will you be preventing the spread of this dis-ease to others, you will be inoculating yourself against this widespread malady. The self-protection you gain will serve you well with another strand of Fungatious Feedback, "Personal Fungatious Feedback," explained in the next chapter.

Chapter 17
Personal Fungatious Feedback

"Self-criticism is how I motivate myself," a colleague once told us. "Self-criticism leads to self-motivation. It's how I get things done."

Some people believe they will be more successful, happy, and effective if they judge, blame, and criticize themselves. Calling themselves fat will help them lose weight because they don't want to see themselves as fat. If they perceive themselves as being lazy, it will help them get moving because they don't want to be lazy. Evaluating their effort as pitiful will motivate them to expend greater effort in the future.

These people think self-putdowns are an expedient way to shift into high gear. They believe if they get after themselves with self-criticism they'll get more done. They think being self-critical blazes a trail to increased achievement.

Wrong. That's not the way it works.

Clearly, self-criticism and self-rejection are effective. They are effective methods to immobilize yourself. If you're busying yourself with generating Personal Fungatious Feedback you're losing time that could be invested in moving forward toward possible solutions, taking constructive action, or implementing positive changes.

Personal Fungatious Feedback definition: A style of communication characterized by disparaging comments to self (self-putdowns) and dwelling on personal weaknesses. Self-talk critical in nature, carrying the silent seeds of inflammation, often leading to stress, doubt, worry and low self-esteem.

Yes, some short-term results might manifest when using self-criticism. Berating yourself with negative words may be the impetus for finishing the report. Calling yourself "chicken" may lead to your asking a woman you're attracted to out on a date. Bludgeoning yourself with self-critical phrases might be the catalyst for painting your bedroom walls.

So what? And big deal! It's possible to paint the bedroom walls without self-criticism. You could ask the woman for a date minus the self-beating you administered in order to summon your courage. You don't need a tirade of negative self-talk to finish the report.

Wait a second! What if it's true? What if you really do need self-criticism (which you don't) to complete the report? The benefits you gain do not equal what you lose. Yes, you gain a finished report. You also end up with diminished self-esteem. You get the bedroom painted, and lose a portion of your self-worth in the process. So maybe she even agreed to go out with you. You gain a date, and you bruise a portion of your fragile self-image.

Achievements such as securing a date, painting a room, and finishing a project are important. Are they as important as how you choose to think about yourself? We think not. Remember, thoughts turn into beliefs and help structure your image of yourself. That image you create will stay with you longer than the time it takes to paint the bedroom.

Using criticism to get after yourself is counterproductive. It uses up your energy and your time. It deters you from focusing on growth, change, and altering unsatisfying situations.

Personal Fungatious Feedback often leads to dis-ease manifesting as depression, discouragement, and fear, which can produce inaction and lower levels of confidence. With depression, the project goes on hold. With discouragement, the painting is likely put off until later. Fear prevents making the phone call.

If constructive change follows self-criticism in your life, it doesn't happen because of it. The constructive change occurs in spite of self-criticism.

At this point, you might be wondering what's wrong with taking a serious look at yourself and working to improve. Nothing. We are in favor of that. And taking that serious look can be done without criticism or putdowns. Self-assessment is always an important step in the change process. Becoming conscious of what we are doing now is the first step toward any meaningful change. Constructive feedback is necessary for giving yourself useful information when considering a new direction. Self-criticism is not. There is a difference.

Throw out self-criticism. Replace it in your mental medicine cabinet with Constructive Feedback. Constructive Feedback, used regularly, produces anti-inflammatory benefits that limit dis-ease and increase personal harmony. *Abracadabra.*

Prescription 1

There are three main ingredients in Constructive Feedback: it's specific, it focuses on behavior, and it delivers information.

"I'm a terrible golfer" is a global statement. It is general in nature and offers no specific information. "I made four putts on two of the holes and three putts on all the others" is specific. It gives you real data to examine.

"I was rude to the customer service representative yesterday." What constitutes "rude" other that a generalized judgment? "Rude" could refer to a hundred different behaviors. "Rude" is an inference that focuses on you as a person rather than on a specific behavior you demonstrated.

"I told her she was stupid and hung up on her."

"I interrupted her three times."

"I stuck my tongue out at her and walked off."

The sentences above fall in the category of Constructive Feedback because they state specific behaviors and give you information to digest. They tell you exactly what you did, minus evaluation, and allow you to decide whether or not you like your behavior.

Prescription 2

Attacks on your personality or character are full of fungi and lower your ability to implement effective change. Practice giving yourself feedback that speaks to the situation rather than to you as a person. Use self-talk that mentions what was done rather than who did it.

"I'm such a slob."

"My memory is terrible."

"What was I thinking?"

"I gave a terrible sales presentation."

"What a fool I am."

The statements above attack your personality or character. Replace them with self-talk that takes the spotlight off the person (you) and shines it on the behavior.

"*I'm* such a slob" now becomes "I spilled my soft drink all over the lunchroom table."

Change "*My* memory is terrible" to "I forgot the two most important parts of my speech."

"What was *I* thinking?" now becomes "I started right out selling and neglected to invest time in building relationship first."

Switch "*I* gave a terrible sales presentation" to "Back-of-the-room sales were lower than anticipated."

"What a fool *I* am" can be improved by saying, "The background check could have been more thorough."

Prescription 3

Be alert for self-talk that describes you as "that way."

"I'm no fun."

"I'm thoughtless."

"I'm not honest."

"I'm a liar."

"I'm uncooperative."

Read the above statements again. How do they resonate with you? Imagine the effect this type of statement has on your well-being, knowing that words create thoughts, which lead to beliefs and influence behaviors.

Change your "I am's" from language that labels you to language that describes your behavior.

"I wasn't much fun to be with during our carpool today."

"I didn't realize how the e-mail would affect her."

"I didn't tell him the truth when I sold him the car."

"I lied about our satisfaction rating."

"I chose not to cooperate with the technology division on that decision."

Maybe you will add these prescriptions to your list of things to do someday soon. Or maybe you would prefer to lament not having cured Personal Fungatious Feedback a year ago. Yet again, you may worry about how others will respond to you if you demonstrate wellness. If so, you are entering unhealthy territory. You have just crossed the line into the land of "Presentphobia."

Chapter 18
Presentphobia

Do people fear the present? One might think so after listening to the plethora of language patterns that focus on the past and/or the future.

"I'm *going to* get after that soon."

"*When* I get my new office I'll organize these files."

"*If only* I had known about that before the meeting."

"*Someday* soon I'm going to tell my manager where to go."

"I *should have* been more precise in my directions."

"*What if* we get there and they call the game because of rain?"

"I *wonder* how she's going to handle that."

The common characteristic of the sentences above is they all announce a decision to live in the past or the future. They are all verbal symptoms of "Presentphobia."

Presentphobia definition: Giving your power away by using language that surrenders present moments. Verbal communications that focus on the dead past or the imagined future. Ignoring the "here and now" reality of our lives.

"This moment is all there is" and "Your only point of power is now" are cute little catch phrases. You hear them and others like them frequently. You see them on posters. Calendars, wall hangings, and bumper stickers showcase their importance. Yet, for all their visibility, these "live in the now" sayings don't seem to have much influence on our everyday language patterns or impact our style of living.

"*What if* she says no?"

"I'm *worried* about her."

"I *hope* he gets the promotion."

"I'll do it *when* I'm older."

"Let's *wait* for a better time."

"I'll tell him *eventually*."

"I'm *going to* start exercising soon."

"I'll be happy *when* we move to the new location."

As the sentences above reflect, you may have the best of intentions about tomorrow. Sorry, even with positive intent it's not possible to be happy, energetic, powerful, or organized tomorrow. Not now. Not during this moment.

"If only *I had listened* to my mother."

"I wish *I had learned* to keyboard better."

"I *should have* saved more money this year."

"Things would be different *if I were* born to richer parents."

"I *ought to have* gone into the field of electronics."

Sorry again. It is not possible to listen to your mother, learn to keyboard, and be powerful yesterday. Yesterday is gone. It's not even a dot on the horizon. It is history.

You know you can only lose weight, improve your spelling, learn to speak Spanish, or be happy NOW. Doing any of those things is not possible one second from now. Nor is it possible to do any of them one second ago. You know there is only one point of power. And you know it is now.

Do you want to hang out in your only moment of power? Do you want to live in the present? Do you want to grab your power and put it to use more effectively in your life? You can only do it now, and your language patterns can help you do just that. Your other choice is to use language that will help you live in the dead past or in the imagined future. You get to decide.

Presentphobia: Futuring

At one of our workshops, Bonnie Kramer, a participant, confessed that she doesn't ever seem to be living in the present. Her thoughts and language contained many symptoms of the futuring aspect of Presentphobia. Paraphrased, this is her story.

- When I carpool to work each morning, my mind thinks about what I will do when I arrive.
- When I get there, my mind drifts to the luncheon meeting and who might be there.
- At lunch, my thoughts center around what I want to complete at my desk in the afternoon.
- During the afternoon session, I notice I'm thinking about what I want to do when I get home.
- During the carpool ride home, I create a plan for dinner.
- While I'm eating, I think of all the things I could do later and what programs are on TV.

- While I'm watching television, I wonder if my husband is going to make sexual advances when we go to bed.
- In bed, my thoughts travel down the road of what to do tomorrow.

It's clear that Bonnie lives a lot of her life in the future. What about you? Are you missing being fully present because of the words and thoughts planted in your consciousness? If you are, the symptoms will show up in your language patterns.

"What if" is one of the main symptoms of futuring. Have you heard yourself say it aloud recently? Perhaps you said it silently to yourself.

"*What if* they show up late?"

"*What if* the machine breaks down?"

"*What if* the recipe doesn't turn out right?"

"*What if* I get sick?"

"What if" statements are an indication that Presentphobia is active in your system. Futuring is a highly contagious strand of Presentphobia and adds to dis-ease in several ways.

1. "What if" keeps you from enjoying your present moments by focusing your energy and attention on an imagined future, one that may never occur.
2. "What if" plants negative pictures in your mind. If you say aloud or silently to yourself, "What if I get sick?" you are likely to picture yourself being sick. An image of being sick often leads to the dis-ease of anxiety, worry, or frustration. Sometimes it leads to being sick.
3. Negative emotional and physical responses can also be triggered by images you create with "what if" statements. If you imagine the recipe not turning out right, you feel the disappointment even though you

have yet to cook the meal. Since the disappointment is already present, you are more likely to choose a different meal or make a mistake following the recipe and end up helping your "what if" become reality.

Prescription 1

Be alert to what you are saying. You can't change something you're unaware of. When you hear the phrase "what if," be advised you could well be living an illusion. The "what if" cue can serve to re-mind you to return to present-moment living.

When you become conscious of a "what if," you can lessen its influence by quickly stating the opposite. If you catch yourself saying, "What if he dislikes my presentation?" follow it immediately with, "What if he loves my presentation?" "What if she gets really upset?" can be overridden with, "What if she gets really happy?"

Prescription 2

An exercise that helps prevent "what if" from entering your language repertoire is what we call the "preposterous probability creation."

Step 1: Pick a goal you desire to complete or an activity you would like to do tomorrow. Possibilities include things like raking the leaves in the yard, finishing your office presentation at home, and planning a winter vacation.

We'll use finishing your office report at home for our example.

Step 2: Now write a couple of "what ifs" that could possibly come true.

Goal: I want to take this report home and finish it there.

- What if my spouse is exhausted and full responsibility for the children goes to me?
- What if traffic is bad and I get home late?
- What if I have to shovel the snow out of the driveway first?

Step 3: Write a few "what ifs" that seem highly unlikely. Create some that have astronomically negative odds of occurring. Add them to your original list.

- What if our house burned down?
- What if I have to go the police station and bail my spouse out of jail?
- What if I have a heart attack on the way home?

Step 4: Now reread your entire list of "what ifs."

- What if my spouse is exhausted and full responsibility for the children goes to me?
- What if traffic is bad and I get home late?
- What if I have to shovel the snow out of the driveway first?
- What if our house burned down?
- What if I have to go the police station and bail my spouse out of jail?
- What if I have a heart attack on the way home?

Realize that none of the "what ifs" on your list are likely to happen. Since none are happening in the present moment, none are real. They are only imagined, a fantasy. If one does occur, you are up to the challenge. You will handle it.

Step 5: Wad up your paper and throw it away. Do it with the energy and satisfaction of a person who just retained his personal power and vanquished the futuring strain of Presentphobia.

Prescription 3

Be on the alert for variations of "what if." "Might" and "could" serve the same purpose of projecting you out of the present moment into the land of imagination.

"She *might* not like my idea for reorganization."

"He *could have* already decided to buy safety equipment from someone else before we get there."

"He *might* reject a cold call."

"The weather *could* turn cold and spoil our day at the beach."

If we were to talk or think with variations of "what if" right now, we could say something like, "People *might* not be interested in this type of book," or "We *could* be wasting our time writing it." If you hear those words come out of one of our mouths, know that we are using up our present moments worrying about an imagined future.

The future of this book is not here yet. Rather than futuring, we can make a healthier choice and use this present time to strengthen the main concepts, edit the manuscript, or create a marketing plan. Those are activities we can engage in now.

If you hear yourself using "might" or "could," stop and review the prescriptions above. Treat all variations of "what if" identically.

Worry Warting

Another strand of Presentphobia occurs when time is invested in worrying. This dis-ease is immobilizing and uses words to create pictures in your consciousness of unpleasant happenings that could occur in the future. Worry is a useless emotion packed full of negative goal setting, expectations, and intentions.

Our friend Willard worried about his teenage son during a recent Friday night. The teen was going to a rock concert with two friends that Willard liked and trusted. Still, he worried. He worried they would drive too fast. He worried about underage drinking. He worried about his son getting mugged. He worried about whether his son would be home on time or not. Willard worried so much that Friday night he lost sleep.

Most of the things we worry about never occur, and that's exactly what Willard experienced. Willard's son did not drive fast. He did not drink or get mugged. He came home on time. Willard's mind-induced insomnia was a waste of his time. Not one thing he worried about came true.

The act of worry warting doesn't prevent what one is worrying about from happening. Had Willard's son and his friends been drinking, no amount of worry on Willard's part would have prevented it. He could have worried for ten straight hours and the worry would not have changed one thing. Whatever the outcome, Willard's worry was all for naught.

An important sidelight to Willard's worry adventure occurred when he used his car to go to the doughnut shop the next morning. He smelled marijuana. It turns out that nothing he worried about occurred, but something he didn't worry about did occur.

When Willard relayed this story to us, he remarked, "I guess I was worrying about the wrong thing." Willard doesn't get it yet. He still believes worrying is valuable. He just believes he was not worrying about the correct issue. He doesn't realize that all worry does is create dis-ease (anxiety, restlessness, insomnia, nervousness) in the mind and body of the worrier.

By worrying, we trick ourselves into believing we're being effective. In reality, we are simply filling our minds and our time with worry which prevents us from doing something constructive. Worry is like sitting in a rocking chair. It gives you something to do, but it doesn't get you anywhere.

Prescription 4

Take action. The main antidote to worry warting is decision making. If there has been no decision made, you provide fertile ground for the spread of worry. When there has been no decision made, the future is unclear, leaving room for worry to enter. When a decision is made, a plan of action usually follows. With a plan in hand, the worrier now has something to do, some action to take. Doing something now inoculates you against worry warting.

Willard found a marijuana smell in his car. He can worry about that if he chooses. Or he can take action. Asking himself, "Is there a decision to be made here?" would be helpful. So would, "Is there something I can do now?" Answering those questions and taking action would likely alleviate the circumstance he is tempted to worry about. When you follow through with action, you jar yourself back to present-moment living. You have effectively reduced Presentphobia in your life.

Hoping and Wishing

Close relatives to worrying are hoping and wishing.

Do you have an employee whose performance is below par? Why not pass the time with hoping and wishing? Hope he improves. Wish it were different. Hope that he resigns. Wish his job performance would get better. That will get you exactly nowhere.

Hoping and wishing serve one major function well. They help you pass time. Time will pass, and things will stay the same. The reality of this cycle is that hopers and wishers actually believe they are using their minds to engage in something worthwhile. They are incorrect.

Hoping and wishing tell your subconscious mind you prefer a certain outcome in the future. By expecting a result in the future, you unconsciously intend for it not to occur now. Since the future never arrives, neither does the result you hoped for. You get what you ask for.

Hoping and wishing produce the dis-ease of pain, frustration, annoyance, and irritation. Hoping and wishing are used to create mental models in your head of how you believe things should be.

"I hope I get a raise."

"I wish I could transfer to the finance division."

"I hope my son applies himself better in school this semester."

With your hopes and wishes firmly planted in your mind, you look out at the world. If it differs from the mental models you created, your reaction could well be disappointment, anger, and hurt. Those unhealthy emotional responses lead to suffering. Do you want to attract more suffering and disappointment into your life? Continue to hope and wish and stay emotionally attached to the outcome.

Prescription 5

Replace hoping and wishing with action. Do something.

"OK, stop right here."

Do you have a question you want to ask, one you've been thinking about for the past couple of pages? We usually get a question at this point, so we're expecting it. Fire away.

"You've been going on and on about not futuring and living in the present. What about planning for the future? If I don't think about or mention the future, how do I complete a plan? How will I accomplish anything without doing some planning?"

We're happy you asked that question. The answer resides in your last phrase, "doing some planning." Planning is doing. *Planning* for the future is not *living* in the future. It is living now. What you are actually doing when you plan is using your present moments to prepare for the future.

Procrastination

One way we prevent ourselves from taking action is through procrastination. We call it the "Sometime Soon Syndrome."

> "*One of these days*, I'll reorganize these files."
>
> "*Eventually*, I'm going to confront him about taking long lunch hours."
>
> "I'm *going to* write a letter to my congresswoman *someday soon*."
>
> "*When* I get more money, I'll start investing."

All of the statements above are examples of postponing. All reflect the Sometime Soon Syndrome. What they all mean is, "I'm putting it off until later." In other words, "I will do nothing NOW." They also mean the communicator is futuring and suffering from Presentphobia.

"I'll do it when . . . " is another Sometime Soon action stopper. Many people use it their entire lives.

I'll do it when I . . .

- graduate.

- get a job.
- save some money.
- finish my master's degree.
- get a promotion.
- become the boss.
- retire.
- write my book.

Each of the responses above is designed to tell others when something will be done. They do not accomplish that goal. What they really tell others is when it will NOT be done. NOW!

People who activate the language of the Sometime Soon Syndrome better be good at waiting. They wait until they have a family, the kids get in school, the spouse goes back to work, the kids attend college, they obtain a divorce, and they remarry.

All are variations of the theme, "I'll do it when my ship comes in." So wait for your ship to come in. Have fun waiting and standing in line. Hope that works for you. Probably not.

Are you happy at work? If not, what are you waiting for?

I'll be happy when . . .

- I get a new office.
- I get a new truck.
- I transfer to another department.
- they paint my office.
- my boss retires.
- we get faster internet service.
- people start listening to me.

There is no end to possible additions to this list. And there is no end to the dis-ease you bring on yourself when you choose this style of speaking, thinking, believing, and acting.

"I'll be happy when" is language that leads you to conclude that happiness is created by outside events. It's no different from "This job makes me happy/mad." If you say, "I'll be happy when I get scheduled on the day shift" often enough, you begin to believe it's the day shift that makes you happy. If you believe that, you have given away your personal power to the concept labeled "day shift."

"I'll be happy when" keeps you focused on the future and thus less powerful in the present. It is an effective way to stay unconscious and give up responsibility for creating happiness right now, in this moment.

Do you prefer to wait until everything is lined up just the way you want it before you take action? Then put "wait" into your language patterns.

Prescription 6

The antidote to procrastination is to get back to "right now."

Replace "I'll be happy when _____ " with "*Right now* I will experience happiness by _____." Change "I'll do it when _____ " to "*Right now* I will do _____ to bring my desire closer."

Then follow through. No waiting allowed.

"Let's *wait* until he calls back."

"I think we better *wait* for the right time."

"Maybe we ought to *wait* until we know for sure."

Remember "I'll do it when . . . "? "Let's wait" is the beginning of another verse of the same song. Both proclaim indecision and inertia. When you use them to announce nonaction, it affects you in two ways. Both are unhealthy. One, by saying, "Let's wait," you provide an excuse for not taking action now. Second, the use of that phrase programs your mind with the mental habit of waiting for certainty.

Yes, there are times when waiting is valuable. Of course there are times when thinking it over, getting another opinion, and letting a situation marinate in your mind for a bit before you make a final decision and take action is valuable.

If you decide to wait for certainty, you could end up waiting a long time. While you were waiting, there's a good chance someone else has already sold the boss on their idea, met with the neighbors to discuss a land dispute, or made the decision on whether or not to invest in the franchise.

You will paralyze yourself if you insist on waiting for certainty before you move off square one. It's another way to overload your present moments with something other than action. And that important something is NOTHING.

Maybe you'll do it eventually.

"*Eventually*, I'll tell her how bad our sales are."

"The new logo will be completed *eventually*."

"I'm *going to* start an exercise program."

"I'm *going to* spend more time with my family."

"Eventually" and "going to" are more of the same procrastination language. Using those words is humming the same tune, the song of the Someday Soon Syndrome.

Prescription 7

Doing is more powerful than *going to*. *Doing now* is more effective than *eventually*. Scrap "going to" and "eventually." If you want to, do it. If you don't want to, don't do it. Both choices reveal more personal power than the wishy-washy "I'm going to."

Many of us have spent excessive amounts of time on futuring. Our Presentphobia manifests when we forecast negative things that might happen to us, wish things were different, wonder what will happen, or describe what we're going to do someday soon. This takes immense amounts of mental energy. Imagine unleashing that energy for living in the present.

"*If only* I knew this stuff when I was younger."

Scrap that line. "If only" belongs in the next section.

Presentphobia: Pasting

Living in the past, or "pasting," is another form of Presentphobia. This dis-ease is brought on by using your present moments replaying, regretting, resenting, and rehashing.

"If only I hadn't gotten married so young."

"I wish I had accepted the offer to go to technology camp."

"I would have liked to have been offered the promotion instead of Carlos getting it."

"Why didn't I realize keyboarding would become so important?"

"We sure had fun before the new regulations were approved."

"I shouldn't have switched vehicles."

All these statements contain language that diminishes your personal power. They use up your present moments by focusing on the past. They immobilize you by concentrating on a dead past that cannot be altered. While you're pasting, you prevent yourself from enjoying the present and using it constructively.

Are you habitually reliving moments that are already over? Do you dispense dis-ease to yourself with regret, guilt, resentment, or lamenting? Not sure? There are clues contained in your language. "If only" is one such clue.

"*If only* I had listened to my gut rather than to my father."

"*If only* I had begun saving twenty years ago."

"If *only* I had patented that idea."

"If *only* I hadn't signed a lease."

Do you enjoy living in the past? "If only" is one phrase that will transport you there quickly. You can use it frequently to stay attached to the past, adding dis-ease to your life and remaining ineffective in the present.

"*If only* she hadn't rejected my proposal."

"*If only* I had franchised this business when I first got the idea."

"*If only* he hadn't turned down my loan application."

"*If only* I had gone to college."

Another nonproductive use of "if only" is procrastination. "If only I had more time, I could write that book" is used to keep you from writing the first page today. "If only the weather forecast was better" is used to prevent you from going through with your picnic plans. "If only the economy would improve" is a way to stall yourself on expansion plans for your business.

"Things would be better if only I had started my own business and worked for myself." Are you sure? Things might be worse. No one knows how things would have turned out if you had begun your own business. You can regret and lament all you want. Still, you will never know for sure.

There are three things you do know for sure: you did not start your own business, she did reject your proposal, and he did turn down your loan application. That is what is. Since that is what is, why not make a healthier use of your present moments by celebrating it? Honor and enjoy what does exist in your life presently. Use this moment to decide what to change, what to do next, what to focus on in this instant.

"If only" isn't the only language technique we use to bring regret and resentment into our lives. There are others.

"Why didn't I see how risky that was?"

"I wish I had taken some business classes in college."

"What was I thinking? How could I have invested in his mall?"

"I would have liked to have been given an opportunity to do the job."

Opportunities lost are the theme of regret played out in the sentences above. When your focus is on opportunities that are gone, the opportunities that exist now are pushed aside. Rehashing the past fills your present moment, and once again you refrain from living fully right now. This sets up the likelihood that you will have things to regret in the future.

When we resent, we leave space for blame to enter. Whether we blame others or ourselves, it's a way to feel bad about things that have already occurred. This mental refighting of an old battle is a no-win situation because the past cannot be changed.

When you use words to hang on tightly to what is over, you only hurt yourself. Wishing you hadn't invested in the mall hurts you, not the person who used your money ineffectively. Wishing you had saved more puts you at dis-ease, not the stockbroker who doesn't even know you exist. It doesn't hurt Carlos that you dwell on the promotion he got instead of you. It fills you with the dis-ease of frustration, annoyance, and believing the world is not fair. He's still walking around feeling fine.

When you are living in regret, how can you see yourself as self-reliant? If your words and thoughts are filled with resentment, how can you perceive yourself as self-confident? Regret and resent and you create a mindset that seeks external justice. That search catapults you back into the belief that outside events, rather than your internal reactions to those events, create your experience.

Another way to invest your present energy by pasting is to use "should have" and "ought to have." Oh, what could have been if you had only done differently!

> "I *should have* worked more closely with him so I could have learned some new skills."
>
> "I *ought to have* been more sympathetic to his complaint."
>
> "I *should have* read this book a long time ago."
>
> "I *ought to have* listened more carefully at the staff meeting."

Do you want to get after yourself with "should have" and "ought to have"? Be our guest. The point is, you didn't. Redoing moments once they have occurred is not possible. Do you want to stay stuck in the past and prevent yourself from taking corrective action or forging a new and bold direction right now? If so, invest your time lamenting how you used moments that are now nothing but history.

Right here, right now, many people wonder, "How can I learn from the past if I don't reflect on it and figure out what I did wrong?" So right here, right now, here is our answer.

Thought, energy, and time invested in looking at past behavior and results, learning from it, and making new choices is useful. As opposed to lamenting the past, serious reflection is a strategy you can use to mobilize yourself for change and growth.

We do not recommend searching the past to determine what you did wrong. Leave right and wrong out of it. What did you do and what results did you create? Was it effective or not? Create a new vision. Make a new plan. Take new action. Move on.

Searching for and finding what you did wrong is a method for creating guilt. Guilt is a useful technique if you want to feel bad. Guilt—anger directed at yourself—puts you at dis-ease, which often hinders helpful action. Guilt keeps you feeling separate from yourself and others. Time you use beating yourself up and feeling guilty is time . . . You know what comes next.

Does guilt change anything you did in the past? No. Does it help you go back and replay it? No. Does it help you change your present behavior? No. If you create change after you do guilt to yourself, that change occurs in spite of guilt, rather than because of it.

Prescription 1

An effective antidote to *should have* is *could have.* Yep, just change "should" to "could."

"I *could have* worked more closely with him" is less judgmental than "I *should have* worked more closely with him."

"I *could have* been more sympathetic to his complaint" is kinder than "I *ought to have* been more sympathetic to his complaint."

"I *could have* listened more carefully at the staff meeting" is descriptive, while "I *ought to have* listened more carefully at the staff meeting" is evaluative.

Once you articulate a "could have," examine it seriously. Decide whether you want to do something or not. For instance, accompany "I could have been more sympathetic to his complaint" with a statement about what you want to do next time. Do you want to be more sympathetic with customers who complain, or not? If you do, state your new desire. "I want to be more sympathetic when customers complain." Vocalizing what you want points you in the direction of growth and change.

Prescription 2

See "If only," "I wish I had," "Why didn't I" and other phrases of lament as a reminder to step forward into present-moment living. When you recognize that signal, stop. Pause and ask yourself, "What can I do in this moment that will impact the situation favorably?" If you identify an appropriate response, implement it. If not, or if you choose not to implement it, refrain from activating regret or resentment. Enjoy the present moment anyway.

Prescription 3

Flush it. Determine your most common "if onlys" and "could haves." Write them on toilet paper and march directly into the restroom. Deposit your writing in the toilet and watch what happens as you flush. A swirl of water will take your "if onlys" and "should haves" and sweep then away and out of sight. Trust they are gone.

The symbolic gesture of flushing the statements will impress on your consciousness the disappearance of the dis-eased words. Do you want to get healthy? Flush sickness down the toilet.

Chapter 19
Degenerative Confidence

How confident are you? Do your language patterns reflect a positive answer? Or do they reveal a degenerating level of confidence? If you're unsure, check it out here. Take the Verbal Confidence Quiz that follows. Mark each item you believe is an indicator of Degenerative Confidence with an X. The answer key is at the end.

1. _____ "I won? This is unbelievable. Incredible."
2. _____ "I better be careful. I might fall."
3. _____ "Close enough."
4. _____ "It was sort of interesting."
5. _____ "I have this little consulting business."
6. _____ "He just called me 'stupid.' That's a rough day he's creating."
7. _____ "That's a bit over my head."
8. _____ "Before I begin, I want to apologize for my voice. I have a cold and it's a little scratchy."

9. _____ "I've told her over a hundred times how happy I am with her."

10. _____ "I ran like the wind today. Ten miles in one hour and forty minutes. I never walked once. I was incredible. I'm a stud."

11. _____ "As Bill Copeland says, 'Try to be like the turtle—at ease in your own shell.'"

12. _____ "I won't like it if the meeting runs overtime."

13. _____ "Don't you think children need to respect their elders?"

14. _____ "When he confirms, I'm going out to dinner to celebrate."

15. _____ "I'm going out to fight the snow now."

16. _____ "Maybe I can do it."

17. _____ "No, I prefer not to."

18. _____ "I'm going to tell Juan Pablo and Celeste about this book."

Answers to the Verbal Confidence Quiz

1. _X_ "I won? This is unbelievable. Incredible."

This is a common response of people who call in to a radio show in an effort to win a prize for being the tenth caller. When they find out they were indeed the winning caller, they say, "I don't believe this is happening to me. This is unbelievable!"

Why would anyone want to say that? Because they don't expect nice things to happen to them, that's why. Their surprise indicates a belief that positive events don't and won't often occur in their lives. They are suffering from Degenerative Confidence.

"Thank you. This is perfect timing. I know exactly what I will do with it. I appreciate your generosity" reveals the confidence of positive expectation and a feeling of self-worth. It is void of dis-ease.

How do you react to your own success and positive occurrences in your life? When you use words like "incredible," "unbelievable," and "amazing," you program yourself to expect less in the future. Expect the best and do not express surprise when it arrives.

2. __X__ "I better be careful. I might fall."

You have received loving warnings your entire life.

"Be careful, you might slip."

"Sit up close or you'll spill food on you."

"You're going to tip that milk over if you're not careful."

Warnings, no matter how well intentioned, plant doubt in your mind. If important people in your life regularly doubt your abilities, you eventually doubt them yourself. Increased doubt results in decreased confidence.

The warnings we are sent from others are disguised expectations. We're warned about spilling our milk by people who expect us to spill our milk. We're warned about falling by people who imagine us falling. With enough repetitions of the warning, we often develop similar expectations of ourselves as well. Our insecurities increase and our confidence wanes.

3. __X__ "Close enough."

Are you interested in shifting your expectations downward and undermining your confidence? The language of mediocrity will help you do that.

"Close enough."

"That'll do."

"It's OK as is."

"A 'C' is average, Dad. It's passing."

If you want to see yourself as a person who settles for less than he wants, use the phrases above. Your expectations will diminish along with your confidence.

Confident people do not settle. They expect the best and they talk in ways that reflect that stance. Tell yourself, "I don't settle." Repeat it often to add confidence and personal power to your life.

When you are tempted to settle, the saying will surface in your consciousness. Listen and follow through. The more often you respond to the message, the more often your mind will send it to you when it's appropriate.

4. <u>X</u> "It was *sort of* interesting."

This verbal construction is an example of watering down your statement. Once again, it weakens your personal power and chips away at your confidence.

"It was *kind of* exciting to see her."

"I *sort of* liked it."

"Kind of" and "sort of" are words of hesitancy. They don't reveal confidence. They hedge the bet. When you use them, you're declining responsibility for your statement.

It was exciting or it wasn't. You liked it or you didn't. Decide, and state your opinion confidently. No water need be added.

5. _X_ "I have this *little* consulting business."

Why do you speak of it as a *little* consulting business? "I have a consulting business" is a more powerful statement. When you qualify it, you erode its strength and your confidence.

"I made some sales *for a change*."

"This is *only* my belief."

"I'm *just* a stay-at-home mom."

When you qualify your statement by telling someone you made some sales *for a change*, you also tell another important person the same thing. You tell yourself. Why not let the "I made some sales" statement stand alone, minus the qualifier?

Listen to the difference as you speak the following statements aloud.

"I made some sales for a change."

"I made several sales this month."

"This is only my belief."

"This is my belief."

"I'm just a stay-at-home mom."

"I'm a stay-at-home mom."

Which messages do you want to feed your belief system?

6. _____ "He just called me 'stupid.' That's a rough day he's creating."

Finally, a statement that doesn't contribute to Degenerative Confidence. There is no X on this one.

Just because someone calls you stupid, fat, or ugly doesn't mean you have to accept it. It matters less what someone says to you and more whether or not you believe it.

You don't get to control what others say about you or how they talk to you. Yes, you can ask to be spoken to in certain ways. You can request that, and the other person still remains in control of how they choose to talk to you. That is not where your power lies.

More important for your confidence and esteem than what someone says to you is what you say to yourself about what they say to you. Your personal power resides in what you say to yourself. Know that when someone calls you stupid, their comment tells more about them than it does about you. Say to yourself, "Wilber must be doing a bad mood today," and retain your strong confidence level.

7. X "That's a bit over my head."

"It's too deep for me."

"I'll never figure it out."

"This is beyond my knowledge base."

Speaking of yourself as unskilled, limited, or incomplete works to build and maintain Degenerative Confidence. The statements above deny capability and focus on perceived limitations. When you talk this way to yourself and others, you build a belief that you are not enough.

Replace talking to yourself as if you are not enough with words that showcase your lack of limits and affirm your completeness.

"I'll figure this one out in a jiffy."

"I'll be able to handle this just fine."

"This is right in my groove."

"I've got this."

"This is a piece of cake for me."

If you're experiencing severe Degenerative Confidence and are uncomfortable saying, "This is right in my groove," or

"I'll be able to handle this," use words that pair a challenging situation with one of your known attributes. "It may take a while, and with my persistence I'll figure it out."

Reject phrases that proclaim doubt.

"I really haven't received any training in this field."

"I doubt this will be easy."

Perhaps you feel unsure when faced with a new experience. In that case, acknowledge your lack of familiarity with the situation and add a comment about your ability to handle the challenge.

"I haven't received any training in this area, and I learn fast."

"I'm unsure about these directions so far. Good thing I'm determined."

8. _X_ "Before I begin, I want to apologize for my voice. I have a cold and it's a little scratchy.

"We can use my office. Don't look around. It's not very clean."

"I'm sorry if this doesn't taste good. It's my first time using this recipe."

Apologizing for yourself preceding an event is a sure sign that Degenerative Confidence is present. It's a clue to others and to yourself that you are unsure, and doubt is making itself known.

This kind of apology doesn't mean, "I'm sorry." It's a manipulative move to influence another's behavior or reaction. It delivers the message, "If I mention it first, you won't be able to, and you might be understanding and lenient with your response."

This style of apologizing takes the blame before anyone else has a chance to find fault. Your degenerating confidence continues to spiral down and leaves you with a lower sense of personal power.

If you catch yourself preparing this type of apology, stop. Ask yourself if you really are sorry. If not, skip the apology.

9. __X__ "I've told her over a hundred times how happy I am with her."

Pure exaggeration is the name we give to the verbal expression above.

"That fish I caught was twenty-six inches long."

"Back in the day, I'd make fifty cold calls every morning."

"There must have been a thousand people there."

When you exaggerate, not everyone knows you're doing it. But *you* do. Did you also know you're admitting to yourself that your thoughts and ideas by themselves aren't enough, that they need help to appear credible? You are reinforcing the belief that your ideas must be surrounded by inflated numbers to have importance. This is another way of telling yourself that you alone are not enough.

Skip the exaggeration. You are enough just the way you are. Adding six inches to the fish, thirty cold calls to your morning, or seven hundred people to the size of the audience are not necessary. We'll say it again. You are enough just the way you are.

10. __X__ "I ran like the wind today. Ten miles in one hour and forty minutes. I never walked once. I was incredible. I'm a stud!"

Closely related to exaggeration, bragging is one more clue that your confidence is low and sinking.

"Look how wonderful I am" is the intended and embedded message delivered with bragging. It spins out of a desire to be enough and the false belief that you aren't. Sadly, the message you send yourself when you brag is, I'm not that wonderful so I better disguise that fact buried in a barrage of words.

Do not confuse bragging with sharing important information about yourself. Talking about your capabilities without exaggeration in a precise, soft-spoken manner is not bragging.

"We are authors. We write books that help parents and educators raise responsible, caring, conscious children." That's giving useful information.

"We are authors of fourteen books containing over 3500 pages. We have helped countless parents and teachers deal with children manifesting behavioral challenges. We have presented our material in seven countries and forty-one states. Most people view us as experts in our field. We are top-of-the-line consultants!" That's bragging.

There is a fine line between bragging and giving useful information. If your words are spoken in a loud or boastful manner, it's bragging. If your intent is to impress or manipulate others, it's bragging. When you deliver a verbal message focused more on giving the other person information they may find useful than on raising your stock in their eyes, it is not bragging.

Do not refrain from sharing interesting and relevant data about yourself. If you do, you will erode your confidence in your own strengths and abilities.

11. __X__ "As Bill Copeland says, 'Try to be like the turtle—at ease in your own shell.'"

According to Thomas Haller, "If you want a behavior, you have to teach a behavior."

Chick Moorman often says, "Nothing is too anything."

Do you consistently quote others? It could be a sign that you are infected with Degenerative Confidence. Turning yourself into a quote machine signals a belief that it's necessary to supplement your words with someone else's.

Quoting others regularly is a clue that you're in denial. You deny your ability to share your opinion without help. You deny the value of sending a message in your own words. You deny that your words, your voice, and you are as valuable as the person quoted.

Quoting others creates a big them/little you stance. It puts the person being quoted above you and ranks their way of speaking above yours.

Hey, you're an expert, too. How could anyone be more qualified than you in describing your beliefs and expressing your thoughts?

When you are about to quote, stop. Answer these questions: Do you feel strongly about what the quote is communicating? Do you believe it? If your answers are yes, put the concept in your own words. Diminish Degenerative Confidence by speaking with the certainty that you alone can best express what is real for you.

12. _X_ "I won't like it if the meeting runs overtime."

We often undermine our confidence with words of prediction.

> "That'll be embarrassing if they announce it in the newsletter."
>
> "I'll be miserable when Monday rolls around again."

"This project will be the death of me."

These anticipated events haven't even occurred yet. Still, the speaker has already activated the mental process that will help create the undesired outcome.

If you say, "I'll be miserable when Monday rolls around again," there is a greater chance you will activate miserable feelings and enact miserable behaviors on Monday.

If you say, "This project will be the death of me," don't be surprised if . . .

How about using predictive language in a positive way? Use words that help you create confident responses to life situations.

> "I'll make it through this and learn a lot in the process."
>
> "Dealing with this conflict will make our company stronger in the end."
>
> "Bring on Monday. I can handle it."

If you're going to be in the business of making predictions, have them strengthen your confidence. Predict success. "I'll get a lot out of reading this book and implementing the concepts" would be a helpful place to start.

13. __X__ "Don't you think children need to respect their elders?"

There are times when a question is not a question. It occurs when someone wants to make a comment and disguises it as a question.

"Don't you think running can hurt your knees?" really means, "I think running will hurt your knees." "Won't that hurt our bottom line in the long run?" is asked by the person lacking the confidence to say, "I believe that is going to hurt our bottom line in the long run."

Say, "I don't feel it's necessary to practice these verbal skills all the time," instead of asking, "Do you really think I need to practice these verbal skills all the time?" When you state your opinion rather than embed it in a question, you sound confident of your opinions, beliefs, and feelings.

14. ____ "When he confirms, I'm going out to dinner to celebrate."

When is the word we recommend you use in place of *if*. "If" breeds doubt and uncertainty. Read the sentences below and see what you think.

"If I get that raise I'll go to Michigan to fish for a week."

"If we hire the new cashier I will cut back on my hours."

"If I get the bonus money I will put it in a retirement account.

Using "when" communicates faith and confidence. It projects positive expectancy and certainty of the outcome. When you act with certainty, you have a better chance of reaching your objective. (Did you notice the "when" in the previous sentence? Stay alert. Here comes another one.) When you stay consciously aware, you increase your odds of speaking, acting, and modeling confidence.

15. _X_ "I'm going out to fight the snow now."

"If you want to be successful, you'll have to *fight* for it."

"Let's go in the boardroom and *wrestle* with that for a while."

"They're slandering us. How shall we *battle* back?"

"You better learn to *fight* for what's yours, son."

"How can we *attack* their new advertising campaign?"

Notice the attack words in the above sentences. They are spoken most often by people who feel threatened and lack confidence. If you think you have to fight for success or battle for what is yours, you must not be sure you'll get it.

If you had high expectations, if you were free of Degenerative Confidence, it would not be necessary to fight. It would not be necessary to put struggle and strain into your language patterns.

People full of confidence don't demonstrate it by loudly proclaiming it using attack vocabulary. Their strength is embodied in their belief in themselves. This inner strength requires no outside verbiage to prop it up.

16. __X__ "Maybe I can do it."

"I'm not sure about that idea."

"Perhaps we will go tomorrow."

"It's possible we'll do that later, Aiden."

This style of language communicates procrastination, indecision, and denial of personal responsibility. It is devoid of confidence.

Degenerative Confidence is thwarted with juicy yes's and no's. "Maybe" packs no punch. It's wishy-washy.

17. ____ "No, I prefer not to."

"Yes, I would love to."

"No, thank you."

"That's not how I want to use my Saturday. I'll pass."

When you say *yes* or *no*, do it fully, without qualifications. If you want to speak confidently without doing guilt or shame to yourself, *no* can stand alone. Excuses, explanations, and reasons for your *no* are not necessary. You get to say *no*.

Fuzzy no's promote Degenerative Confidence. When they're used, the other person isn't sure whether you said no or not. Have you ever had an exchange like this?

"Would you like to go to a movie with me Friday night?"

"I have to see my tax preparer that night."

Where do you stand now? Do you ask about another night? Do you back off? The fuzzy no doesn't give you much valuable information, does it?

The person asked you if you would *like* to go, not if you *could* go to the movies. When your answer tells the questioner that you're busy, you didn't answer the question that was asked.

If you get a request and don't want to accept, send a polite, juicy no. "No, thank you" or "I'd prefer not to" are clear, honest replies. They leave no doubt with the receiver.

If you would like to accept the request and already have other plans, use a juicy answer. "I'd love to go to a movie, and I have a tax appointment Friday night. Is there another night we could do it?"

If you are hesitant to say no, you might be suffering from the false belief system that says you can hurt another's feelings. We covered that in Chapter 2. When you get clear in your mind that other people can be hurt only when they choose to be, it will become easier for you to say no. Until then, you will likely attempt to control their emotional reactions. When you are willing to let others be in charge of their own feelings, you will more often make decisions based on whether or not you really want to accept an invitation or request and less on how the other person might choose to feel if you say no.

Juicy yes's and juicy no's are kind to the other person. You have given them the kindest message of all, the truth.

When you say yes, also do it fully, without qualifications. Say yes and mean it. If you say yes and you really wanted to say no, you will most often end up resenting that you didn't say what you meant.

Do you desire to grow your confidence as a decision maker? Say yes only when you can follow through with energy, excitement, and enthusiasm.

18. ____ "I'm going to tell Juan Pablo and Celeste about this book."

What does this have to do with Degenerative Confidence? We are confident you will be willing to share the valuable concepts in this book with the important people in your life. Right?

Was that a yes or a no?

Prescription 1

To put more confidence in your life, speak confidently. Pick any one of concepts 1-18 and begin integrating it into your verbal repertoire. It doesn't matter where you begin. It does matter that you *do* begin. If you aren't feeling confident, talk as if you are.

Prescription 2

Act confident. Your mind is impressed with actions. When you act as if you're confident, you're more likely to be seen as confident. You will also strengthen your view of yourself as a confident person.

Take action, change your words, remind yourself of your emerging confidence, and you will steadily reduce Degenerative Confidence.

Conclusion

Words.
Words structure thoughts.
Thoughts build beliefs.
Beliefs lead to actions.
Abracadabra.

That's all. Except there is more.

Change your words and you change your thoughts.
Change your thoughts and you change your beliefs.
Change your beliefs and you change your behaviors.
Change your behaviors and you change your world.
Change your world and you change our world.
Change our world and you change *the* world.
Almost like magic.

The situation you find yourself in right now you created with words, thoughts, and deeds. Want to change your situation? Change your words, thoughts, and deeds.

Like pulling a rabbit out of a hat.

We, Chick and Thomas, are self-made linguists. We believe in the power of words. So do you, on some level, or you wouldn't have read this far. We assume you are serious about implementing the language of personal power, self-responsibility, and conscious awareness. We assume you care deeply about eliminating the 13 verbally transmitted diseases in your own life and in the lives of your significant others. To that end, we offer twenty do's and don'ts to consider when implementing the important concepts contained in this book.

1. **Do get started now**. If you haven't already, get moving on creating healthy language habits for yourself. It doesn't matter if you have read a book, attended a full-day seminar, or invested two days learning how to tile your bathroom floor. The sooner adult learners do any one new thing they learned, the greater the chance they will do more. The longer adult learners wait before they do any one new thing they learned, the greater the chance they will do nothing. Do something today.

2. **Do be selective**. Working to implement every concept in this book simultaneously is not realistic. Pick one or two language skills to work on. You know which ones. As you achieve mastery in those, move on to others.

3. **Do use file cards**. Write a language concept on a file card. Keep it in your pocket. Every time you become

aware of the card, practice the concept. You can keep cards on your mirror, at your desk, or on the dashboard of your car. They serve as useful reminders that you are serious about creating a new mind with new language.

4. **Do pay attention**. If you fail to hear or notice unhealthy language, you are powerless to do anything about it. Once you notice your words or thoughts, you take the wheel of control and can shape your future. Monitor your self-talk when you get out of bed in the morning. Invest some time noticing your inner dialogue. Resist judging it. Simply notice your thoughts as they come and go. The goal here is to notice, not evaluate. You are practicing paying attention. After you have paid attention to your inner dialogue in the morning for a couple of weeks, tune into your language patterns as you drive the car, jog, or work on an office project. Especially tune into those times you feel caught up in strong emotion.

5. **Don't try**. Trying doesn't work. Doing does. Trying is a cop-out. "I'm going to try to change my language" is a signal that you have set yourself up to be unsuccessful. "Well, I tried," you can tell yourself later. No, just do it. Now.

6. **Do find a compatriot**. The people you have currently attracted into your life may not understand your effort to eliminate dis-ease by changing your words, thoughts, and beliefs. You were vibrating with one kind of energy when you found them. By changing your words and thoughts you will be changing the energy that brought you together. You may want to

locate a person on a similar path, someone you can talk to with your emerging language patterns, someone to celebrate with, someone who will understand and affirm your new style of speaking. And you can do the same for them.

7. **Do use journals and give yourself assignments**. These can take the form of intentions, goals, or a contract. Be specific, and record them in writing. "I intend to use descriptive praise five times today." "I will use 'and' instead of 'but' when I write my report this afternoon." By concentrating on one or two specific assignments, you will reduce the diluting effect of attempting to do many at once. A language journal will help you keep track of your progress. You can also note any self-talk or talk from others that occurs during your implementation effort.

8. **Don't judge where you are on the implementation path**. Skill acquisition follows sequential stages. Honor the stage you are currently at and celebrate it.

   Stage One is *unconsciously unskillful*. That's where you are when you're so unskillful you aren't even aware that you're unskillful. Many of you reading this book began at that step. You didn't even know there were verbally transmitted diseases. If so, let that be OK.

   Stage Two is *consciously unskillful*. Perhaps as you were reading this book you became aware that you were unskillful in your language selection. That's an important step. It signifies you are no longer unconscious. It's difficult to make growth moves if you're unconscious. So now you are conscious. Congratulations. Celebrate that.

During this time, you will experiment with new words and phrases. At this stage you may experience your new language attempts as awkward or phony. The sense of awkwardness stems from its newness. It doesn't sound familiar yet. Rejoice. This is a signal you are crossing from Stage Two to Stage Three.

In Stage Three, *consciously skillful*, you will find you are skillful when you're consciously thinking about how you are speaking or thinking. When you purposefully and intentionally make an effort and rehearse your intentions, your language skills will be more precise. Keep working on being skillful consciously and you will eventually move to Stage Four, *unconsciously skillful*.

Unconsciously skillful is where you don't purposefully think about your language anymore. You simply speak with healthy, self-responsible, dis-ease-free language without even thinking about it. You are so skilled at this stage that your language becomes unconscious again.

9. **Do be persistent**. Nurture yourself with positive self-talk as detailed in these pages and eventually you will reach Stage Four. There is no set time to begin walking or using a spoon correctly. Likewise, there is no specific time when people will learn to use healthy, self-responsible language. Take your time if you choose. And hang in there.

10. **Don't try to change others**. Yes, there are coworkers, relatives, and friends you thought about often as you read these pages. You thought about them and wished they would apply some of these concepts in their lives. You know just which concepts would benefit which people. These people are NOT prime candidates to become your students. The problem with working to change the language patterns of people *you* think need it is *they* don't think they need it.

    If you're serious about helping significant people in your life eliminate the 13 verbally transmitted diseases from their lives, concentrate on yourself. Master these concepts yourself and put them to use regularly. Model the concepts and these important people may notice. If you stop teaching, they may start learning from watching and listening.

11. **Don't correct another's language**. "No, I am not hurting your feelings. You are choosing to hurt yourself. Only you can do that to yourself." Reminding people of the "Makes Me" Psychosis or any other verbal dis-ease is not effective when people are in the midst of strong emotion. Instead, lead with empathy and concentrate on listening. "I hear how much you are hurting. I'm sorry you feel that way. Say some more."

12. **Do explain to your children and spouse your new language goals and their significance**. Your main job as a parent is to keep your children healthy and safe. This includes the dangers that dis-eased language patterns present. Protect your family from the threat of verbally transmitted diseases the same way you would

protect them from sexually transmitted diseases, through information, explanations, and modeling. Speak self-responsible language in their presence. Give explanations for how and why you are talking the way you do. Self-responsible language can become your family's language of choice.

13. **Don't overreact to the reactions of others**. "Stop talking to me that way. You're using a technique on me. You are not my therapist." "You are making me mad. In fact, you're making me even madder right now." These words are signals to back off. You are waving a red flag in front of a bull. There is a better time than this to discuss the issue rationally. Be the adult in the room. Return to the issue later.

14. **Do take control of how you hear what others say**. While you cannot always control how others talk to you, you can always control how you hear how they talk to you. When your boss says "but" in a sentence or written evaluation, mentally change it to "and." If your spouse says, "I *need* some time with you," hear "I *want* some time with you." When your coworker informs you he will *try* to have the material to you by the end of the day, hear what he's really saying: "I'm probably not going to have that material to you today." Plan accordingly or make other choices.

15. **Do exercise your language muscles**. If you don't use it, you lose it. Tone up those vocal cords with regular practice. Not exercising your language muscles is as unhealthy as not exercising your body. Don't settle for flabby language. Get off the couch and put those muscles to regular use. Think of it as *innercise*. Just as

physical exercise keeps your exterior in shape, *innercise* will lead you to inner fitness.

16. **Do not choose frustration**. The default system of our culture is unself-responsible language. Roll with the punches. If you're in France, people are going to speak French. No amount of wishing and hoping they'll speak English is going to change that. When you're in France, French is the language of choice. When you're in English-speaking cultures, unself-responsible language is the language of choice. Know that if you are speaking self-responsible language, you are speaking a foreign language.

17. **Do lighten up**. Enjoy your mistakes. You will make some. If you're not striking out occasionally, you aren't swinging at enough pitches. When you risk using this language in public, you win. You win by doing it perfectly or you win by gaining valuable data you can put to use next time.

18. **Don't hope for results**. Expect them.

19. **Do choose the people you surround yourself with wisely**. If you're looking for a spouse, therapist, doctor, friend, or employee, look for someone who is not spreading dis-ease. You do not want a doctor who tells you, "*If* you make it two years you're home free." You want a doctor who says, "*When* you make it two years you're home free." Do not choose a therapist who *shoulds* on you. Pick a spouse who *wants* you rather than one who *needs* you. If you have a choice between an employee who says, "I *can't* keyboard

that fast," and one who says, "I *don't* keyboard that fast, *and* I am a fast learner," you know who to pick.

20. **Do pass it on**.

One Last Word

Together, we can heal the world one person, one day at a time.

Today can be your day.

Today you can be the person.

Isn't it your turn to be the one?

About the Authors

Chick Moorman

Chick Moorman is the director of the Institute for Personal Power, a consulting firm dedicated to providing high-quality professional development activities for educators and parents.

He is a former classroom teacher with over fifty years of experience in the field of education. His mission is to help people experience a greater sense of personal power in their lives so they can in turn empower others.

Chick conducts full-day workshops and seminars for school districts and parent groups. He also delivers keynote addresses for local, state, and national conferences.

He is available for the following topic areas:

FOR EDUCATORS

- The Teacher Talk Advantage
- Motivating the Unmotivated
- Achievement Motivation and Behavior Management through Effective Teacher Talk
- Celebrate the Spirit Whisperers
- Teaching Respect and Responsibility

FOR PARENTS

- Parent Talk: Words That Empower, Words That Wound
- The Only Three Discipline Strategies You Will Ever Need
- The 10 Commitments: Parenting with Purpose
- Empowered Parenting

If you would like more information about these programs or would like to discuss a possible training or speaking date, please contact:

Chick Moorman
P.O. Box 547
Merrill, MI 48637
Telephone: 877-360-1477 (toll free)
Fax: 989-643-5156
E-mail: ipp57@aol.com
www.twitter.com/chickmoorman
www.facebook.com/chick.moorman
Websites: www.chickmoorman.com and
www.uncommon-parenting.com

Thomas B. Haller, MDiv, MSW, ACSW, DST

Thomas Haller is a parenting and relationship specialist, the coauthor of seven highly acclaimed books, a psychotherapist maintaining a private practice (for 25 years) as a child, adolescent, and couples therapist, a sex therapist, and a chronic pain counselor. He is a Certified Master Forensic Social Worker, an AASECT certified diplomate of sexuality therapy, a certified EEG biofeedback technician, and a certified sports counselor.

Thomas is the chief parenting and relationship correspondent to WNEM TV 5 (CBS affiliate). He has been the weekly radio personality for several years on Mid-Michigan's number one radio station, WCRZ 107.9FM. Thomas has also been a featured guest on over 150 radio shows, including such notable programs as Oprah Radio, Playboy Radio, and the World Puja Network.

In addition, Thomas is the founder and director of the Healing Minds Institute, a center devoted to teaching others to focus and enhance the health of the mind, body, and spirit. He is president of Personal Power Press, Inc., a publishing house committed to providing parents and educators with practical material for raising responsible children. Thomas and his wife Valerie maintain a not-for-profit 501 (c) (3) organization, Healing Acres, an equine retirement ranch enabling aged horses to live out their lives in a low-stress environment.

Thomas is available for workshops, seminars, student assemblies, and commencement speeches.

Website: www.thomashaller.com
Twitter: www.twitter.com/tomhaller
Facebook: www.facebook.com/thomas.b.haller
Blog: www.uncommon-parenting.com
E-mail: Thomas@thomashaller.com

Thomas on television answering viewer questions:

Family Matters Segment – Every Wednesday at 12:15 p.m. on WNEM TV5 News at Noon
Family Matters Segment – Every Saturday at 8:45 a.m. on WNEM TV5 Weekend Wake-up
Family Matters Segment – Every Sunday at 7:45 & 8:45 a.m. on WNEM TV5 Weekend Wake-up
Relationship Matters Segment – Every Monday at 9:00 a.m. on WNEM TV5 Better Mid-Michigan
Past segments can be viewed online at www.wnem.com

Thomas on the radio answering questions and discussing hot topics:

Every Thursday morning at 7:30 a.m. on WCRZ 107.9FM – Streaming live online at www.wcrz.com

Other Books and Products

www.personalpowerpress.com

For Educators

THE TEACHER TALK ADVANTAGE: Five Voices of Effective Parenting, by Chick Moorman and Thomas Haller ($24.95)

SPIRIT WHISPERERS: Teachers Who Nourish a Child's Spirit, by Chick Moorman ($24.95)

TEACHER TALK: What It Really Means, by Chick Moorman and Nancy Weber ($15.00)

TEACHING THE ATTRACTION PRINCIPLE TO CHILDREN: Practical Strategies for Parents and Teachers to Help Children Manifest a Better World, by Thomas Haller and Chick Moorman ($24.95)

SPIRIT WHISPERERS IN ACTION eBook, by Chick Moorman and Thomas Haller ($11.95)

For Parents

PARENT TALK ESSENTIALS: How to Talk to Kids about Divorce, Sex, Money, School and Being Responsible in Today's World, by Chick Moorman and Thomas Haller ($15.00)

PARENT TALK: How to Talk to Your Children in Language That Builds Self-Esteem and Encourages Responsibility, by Chick Moorman ($15.00)

THE ONLY THREE DISCIPLINE STRATEGIES YOU WILL EVER NEED: Essential Tools for Busy Parents, by Chick Moorman and Thomas Haller ($14.95)

TEACHING THE ATTRACTION PRINCIPLE TO CHILDREN: Practical Strategies for Parents and Teachers to Help Children Manifest a Better World, by Thomas Haller and Chick Moorman ($24.95)

THE LANGUAGE OF RESPONSE-ABLE PARENTING, audiocassette series featuring Chick Moorman ($39.50)

PARENT TALK FOCUS CARDS, by Chick Moorman ($10.00)

DENTAL TALK: How to Manage Children's Behavior with Effective Verbal Skills, by Thomas Haller and Chick Moorman ($24.95)

THE 10 COMMITMENTS: Parenting with Purpose eBook, by Chick Moorman and Thomas Haller ($11.95)

THE PARENT TALK TIP COLLECTION: 730 Practical Verbal Skills to Help You Raise Responsible, Caring, Conscious Children eBook, by Chick Moorman and Thomas Haller ($7.95)

For Couples

COUPLE TALK: How to Talk Your Way to a Great Relationship, by Chick Moorman and Thomas Haller ($24.95)

Qty.	Title	Price Each	Total
		Subtotal	
		Tax (MI residents 6%)	
		S/H (See chart below)	
		Total	

Please add the following shipping & handling charges:
$1 - $15.00 -- $4.95 $15.01 - $30.00 -- $5.95
$30.01 - $50.00 -- $6.95 $50.01 and up 15% of total order
Canada: 30% of total order. US funds only, please.

Ship To:

Name: ______________________________

Address: ______________________________

City: ______________ State: ______ Zip: ___________

Phone: ______________________________

☐ **American Express** ☐ **Discover** ☐ **VISA** ☐ **MasterCard**
☐ **Check/Money Order (payable in US funds)**
Card #: _________-__________-__________-__________

Expiration Date: _______/________

Signature: ______________________________

PERSONAL POWER PRESS, INC.
P.O. Box 547, Merrill, MI 48637
Phone: (877) 360-1477 - Fax: (989) 643-5156 - E-mail:
customerservice@personalpowerpress.com
www.personalpowerpress.com

Newsletters

Chick Moorman and Thomas Haller publish FREE e-mail newsletters for parents and educators. To subscribe to either of them, e-mail: customerservice@personalpowerpress.com

Or you can visit: www.personalpowerpress.com

Blog

Uncommon Parenting Blog: www.uncommon-parenting.com